The Applause Musical Library

Sweeney Todd
The Demon Barber of Fleet Street

MUSIC AND LYRICS BY
STEPHEN SONDHEIM

BOOK BY
HUGH WHEELER

FROM AN ADAPTATION BY CHRISTOPHER BOND

INTRODUCTION BY
CHRISTOPHER BOND

THEATRE BOOK PUBLISHERS

Grateful acknowledgement is made to the following for permission to include their photographs and scene and costume designs: Van Williams, Martha Swope Associates/Carol Rosegg, Zoë Dominic Photography, Eugene Lee and Franne Lee.

Drawings by Hirschfeld Copyright © 1979, 1989 by Al Hirschfeld and reproduced by special arrangement with Hirschfeld's exclusive representative, The Margo Feiden Galleries Ltd., New York.

Design by Gary Denys.

Library of Congress Cataloging-in-Publication Data
Sondheim, Stephen.
  [Sweeney Todd. Libretto]
  Sweeney Todd, the demon barber of Fleet Street / music and lyrics by Stephen Sondheim ; book by Hugh Wheeler ; based on an adaptation of Sweeney Todd by Christopher Bond ; introduction by Christopher Bond.
    p. cm. — (Applause musical library)
  Libretto of a musical.
  Discography: p.
  ISBN 1-55783-065-7 :   —ISBN 1-55783-066-5 (pbk.)
    1. Musicals–Librettos. I. Wheeler, Hugh. II. Bond, C. G. (Christopher Godfrey), 1945- Sweeney Todd.
III. Title. IV. Series.
ML50.S705S9   1990   <Case>   90-40265
782.1'4'-0268–dc20   CIP
                                                                                                    MN

Applause Theatre & Cinema Books
19 West 21st Street, Suite 201
New York, NY 10010
Phone: (212) 575-9265
Fax: (212) 575-9270
Email: info@applausepub.com
Internet: www.applausepub.com

Sales & Distribution:
Hal Leonard Corp.
7777 West Bluemound Road
P.O. Box 13819
Milwaukee, WI 53213
Phone: (414) 774-3630
Fax: (414) 774-3259
Email: halinfo@halleonard.com
Internet: www.halleonard.com

Applause books are available through your local bookstore, or you may order at www.applausepub.com or call Music Dispatch at 800-637-2852.

First Applause Printing, 1991

"Sweeney Todd,
The Demon Barber of Fleet Street"
was originally produced on Broadway by
Richard Barr, Charles Woodward,
Robert Fryer, Mary Lea Johnson, Martin Richards

CONTENTS

INTRODUCTION

For me there is only one rule in the theater: Does it work? And by that I don't mean will the show run for twenty years or make X million dollars, but have I come out of the theater feeling more alive than when I went in? Has my imagination been fired, my emotions been aroused, my brain kick-started into life? Is my heart pounding and my mind racing; and, if the show is a musical, do a series of discordant and Neanderthal groans issue from my mouth? (This is known as Chris hums the score.) When I see *Sweeney Todd* all these things usually happen.

My involvement with the show goes back to 1968—I wrote the play on which Stephen Sondheim based his musical, have directed four productions of the musical in England and Scandinavia, and seen a further six or seven productions around the world. What follows is a highly subjective and partial history that will almost certainly be inaccurate in places—I am writing this entirely from memory as I am in Sweden directing a show and have no access to any notes, diaries, books, or records. A perfect opportunity to be a theater critic for a day and try to force the facts to fit my own prejudices . . .

HISTORY

Sweeney Todd is pure fiction. Plenty of unhinged and vindictive malcontents have worked in Fleet Street over the last two hundred years (until very recently most English newspapers had their offices there), but no one has ever succeeded in finding a shred of evidence as to the existence of a Demon Barber thereabouts. There was one in revolutionary Paris—a Jacobin who cut his customers' throats, though whether for profit or because of political differences is unclear. In seventeenth-century Scotland there are accounts of a family of robbers led by one Sawney Bean who are said to have eaten their victims. Shakespeare's Titus Andronicus kills and bakes two brothers in a pie before serving them up to their mother, Tamora, Queen of the Goths; and every culture has tales of cannibalism from the Gilgamesh of Babylon through Transylvania to the present day. Some would claim that a benign form of cannibalism remains with us in ritualized form in the communion service of the Catholic Church.

It's against this background that Sweeney Todd started life in the 1830s in London. He was the creation of George Dibden-Pitt, a freelance journalist who wrote an account of Sweeney's life and crimes for a "penny dreadful," a broadsheet that sold for a penny and was roughly equivalent to the more preposterous of our present-day tabloids. "Aliens Bonked My Mother-in-Law!" "Vicar Eats Royal Gerbil—Shock Horror!" etc. Sweeney was a psychopath who killed for profit and Mrs. Lovett a harridan who baked the bodies. The story was widely believed to be true, and aroused such interest that George immediately adapted it for the stage, where it became an instant success.

MELODRAMA

The theaters George's play was performed in were known as "Blood Tubs" on account of the fact that their repertoire was almost exclusively devoted to shows of the most lurid and sensational kind. Large helpings of sex and violence, with a perfunctory spoonful of Christian humbug at the end. The atmosphere these shows were performed in

2

was rough and boisterous, and whilst we can speculate on the standard of the performances when measured against today's menu at the bourgeois culture trough, there is no doubt that they possessed at least some of the essential ingredients that go to make good theater: energy and commitment crackling between the stage and the audience; involvement; passion and fun. Nowadays the word *melodrama* is usually used pejoratively, as if there were something inherently cheap and phony about it, and modern revivals usually seek to poke fun at the form rather than attempt to get to grips with the subject matter. Such exercises seem to me to be pointless and depressing; mocking and distorting the past may make us feel superior, but it can give us no understanding of the present. Having said that, there is no doubt that on the printed page most melodramas seem lifeless and stilted and give very few clues as to how they must have been in action. And the original script of *Sweeney Todd* is no exception.

THE PLAY

In 1968 I was working as an actor at the Victoria Theatre, Stoke-on-Trent, an excellent repertory theater in the Midlands—the center of England. The theater announced *Sweeney Todd* as a forthcoming attraction; no one had read the script but another melodrama, *A Ticket-of-Leave Man,* had been a success two seasons before, and we thought that if the script needed doctoring we could sort it out in rehearsals. Due to a series of cock-ups we didn't get hold of a copy of the play until two weeks before rehearsals were due to begin, and on the page the show was crude, repetitive, and simplistic—hardly any plot and less character development. It didn't need doctoring, it needed a heart transplant. And preferably new lungs and balls as well. I had had a novel published the year before and with the optimism/arrogance of youth (I was twenty-three), cheerfully volunteered to write my first play: It would retain the title, the razors, the pies, and the trick chair and be delivered in a week's time. Fortunately it wrote itself. I crossed Dumas's *The Count of Monte Cristo* with Tourneur's *The Revenger's Tragedy* for a plot; added elements of pastiche Shakespeare in a sort of blankish verse for Sweeney, the Judge, and the lovers to talk; borrowed the name of the author of *The Prisoner of Zenda* for my sailor boy; remembered some market patter I'd learnt as a child; and adapted the wit and wisdom of Brenda, who ran the greengrocer's shop opposite my house, for Mrs. Lovett's ruminations upon life, death, and the state of her sex life. I met my deadline with a couple of hours to spare and started rehearsals playing Tobias Ragg, which I'd written for myself, a week later. The show was well received and was subsequently produced several times in various theaters in England, and eventually, due to the efforts of my agent, Blanche Marvin, at the Theatre Royal, Stratford East in London in the mid-seventies. It was there that Stephen Sondheim saw it. And perhaps that's where the real story begins because whilst I have great affection for the play, until Steve performed his alchemical miracle on it, it remained a neat pastiche that worked well if performed with sufficient panache, but base metal nevertheless. But the transformation to pure gold was about to begin.

SONDHEIM

Blanche told me that someone named Stephen Sondheim had seen the show—I'm ashamed to say I'd never heard of him at that time. There had been talk of doing the play in New York, but the American producers who were interested in the project, Richard Barr and Charles Woodward, were now asking if we would be willing to shelve that idea in favor of a possible musical that Steve would write. Blanche was very enthusiastic about the idea. I took her advice. I remember two meetings round about that time but can't remember which order they came in.

I think the first was with Steve's agent, Flora Roberts, and I'm fairly certain I was drunk (a semi-permanent state until 1984 when I knocked it on the head and joined AA). I remember being terrified of her (I still am) and thinking that she reminded me of a cross between Mae West and a New York version of Lady Bracknell. She was extremely direct and straightforward and in attempting to match these qualities I swore a lot and ended up by saying (expletives deleted): "Look, if he [Steve] is any good, and she [Blanche] says he is, then let him do what he likes with it [my play]." Which with the benefit of hindsight is one of the more spectacularly sensible things I've said in my life.

The other meeting was with Steve at the Granada studios in Manchester where they were filming numbers from *Side by Side by Sondheim* for TV. I was moving house at that time, and, since I was driving a large lorry full of furniture, was sober for once. We talked about the play in some detail and what struck me most forcibly was his complete lack of bullshit. "What a lovely bloke," I remember thinking. "What's he doing working in the theater?" I find it difficult to write about someone whom I admire so much without it sounding soppy; suffice it to say that since I've become familiar with his work I find it difficult to sit through a show that isn't by Stephen Sondheim without wishing that it was. I have also been known to pick fist-fights with people who complain that his work has no heart. For their information the heart is a large and powerful muscle that pumps blood, a singularly inappropriate organ to tie up in a pink ribbon or fit with a neat attachment for wearing on the sleeve. And from "Being Alive" to "No One Is Alone" and at all points in between I hear the double thump of a heart as big as a house. And if in *Sweeney* the blood it pumps is sometimes black with bile it nevertheless remains hot, strong, and foaming with life. Steve has always been generous about my contribution to *Sweeney*: it's nice to be able to say thanks.

THE MUSICAL

Steve's original intention was to write a sung-through show without dialogue, but when this proved impractical he approached Hugh Wheeler, with whom he had collaborated on previous shows, including *A Little Night Music* and *Pacific Overtures*, to write the book for the show. It's no secret that Hugh Wheeler and I had our differences: professional rather than personal, but since he died in 1987 I don't feel it's appropriate to discuss them here as there were doubtless faults on both sides, and he's unable to put his point of view. What is indisputable is that *Sweeney Todd* is a book-heavy musical. Its storyline and character development run directly parallel to those in the play; the plot and subplots are complicated and all major characters interlock and interrelate. Indeed, were one feeling pretentious one could even subtitle the piece *Aspects of Love*, for that is what everyone in the show is looking for. It is Sweeney's love for his wife and daughter that sustains him through his fifteen-year exile and brings him back to London; it is Mrs. Lovett's love for Sweeney that makes her keep his razors and forges anew their fatal partnership. Judge Turpin and Anthony both love Johanna in their different ways; and Johanna reciprocates. The Beggar Woman once loved and now "loves" professionally. Tobias has never known love but desires it above all else. Add to all this Sweeney's relationship with his razors and Mrs. Lovett's with the coin of the realm and you have just about covered the entire spectrum from necrophilia through rape and filial duty to romance. We care about the characters in *Sweeney* because they care so passionately about each other; and on a good night we plunge headlong to triumph and disaster with them. The music sees to that.

I'm not competent to comment on the score (I've been known to ask a conductor if he could cut three and a half bars of Verdi to help me stage an aria; when the wind is from the north I can still feel a piece of his baton lodged somewhere up my left nostril) beyond saying that for me it perfectly mirrors and distills the particular people and precise situations in the show. And lifts them to another plane.

SWEENEY *IN PERFORMANCE*

My only quarrel with Hal Prince's original Broadway production at the Uris Theatre is that it was at the Uris Theatre. It seems a strange place to tell stories in; and that's what we do, isn't it? But then I have very seldom enjoyed a show in a venue that seats many more than a thousand people. A lot depends upon the architecture, but generally speaking if you go much beyond that number I find it difficult to get involved in what's happening. The sets get larger, the amplification gets greater, the hype begins, the tickets get more expensive to pay for it all, the hype increases, and eventually the event begins to take on all the subtlety and humanity of a Roman circus. Theater is a personal and human activity and I think it's usually best on a human scale. It's a tribute to everyone concerned with the original production that it worked so brilliantly, but I've always felt it did so in spite of, rather than because of, where it opened.

As with any worthwhile and complex show there are many ways of interpreting it and balancing its component parts. There is no right or wrong way, only, "Does the end result add up to a graphic realization of the authors' intentions? Does it successfully tell their story here and now?" Within these parameters directors, designers, actors, and technicians make the choices that give their particular production its particular emphasis and dynamics. What follows are some highly personal preferences.

The people in *Sweeney* are fuelled by basic and simple

human emotions: greed, lust, vengeance, and a desire to love and be loved in return. They inhabit a corrupt, unjust, and dangerous world, but this should tend to intensify their humanity rather than destroy it. To overemphasize the elements of the show encapsulated most clearly in the lines:

"The engine roared, the motor hissed,
And who could see how the road would twist . . .?"

is in some ways to deny the audience's total involvement with the people and events in the story, and is ultimately too Brechtian an approach for me. If the people are dehumanized for any reason we cease to care about them. Paradoxically, when I have directed the show I have always shifted the emphasis of the first two scenes of Act II by having grotesquely frock-coated and crinolined figures in half-masks as Mrs. Lovett's customers and Sweeney's anonymous victims because I don't want people involved with them. Visually, this ties up with the dumb-show rape of Sweeney's wife in Act I, and I like the idea that the pie shop and barber shop have become a chic venue for the gentry to attend—the white folks slumming it in Harlem, so to speak. The masks also seem to fit well with Sweeney's almost dreamlike state during the "Quartet" and maybe add another layer of meaning to the line:

"Those above will serve those down below . . ."

The other major shift that I have attempted in production is in the middle section of Act I. The first act is very long and it was found necessary in the original production to cut the Judge's song; this seems unfortunate as it tends to reduce him to an all-purpose baddie, and I have found it more satisfactory to introduce Anthony into the market scene to get across swiftly such plot points as are important, follow the market scene with the Judge's song, and then cut almost the entire scene in the barber's shop up to Pirelli's entrance, retaining just enough lines to reestablish the Beggar Woman's presence in the street and Sweeney's growing impatience that the Beadle has not yet come for a shave. It is also possible to keep Pirelli's song in the market intact; it is long, but if the scene can be staged so that he sings as he shaves and pulls teeth, then it holds.

These and other minor alterations I made when I first directed the show at the Liverpool Playhouse in 1981. With a cast of ten and an orchestra of five. Which I think is the minimum it should be attempted with! I think it worked: It certainly did for the punter who, when Sweeney's razor was poised over the disguised Johanna's neck, leapt to his feet and yelled: "Don't kill 'er, yer soft get; she's yer daughter!" He subsequently became aware of where he was and sat down in confusion. But maybe melodrama isn't completely dead and buried. I hope not. Now read on. Bon Appetit.

Chris Bond

Karlstad, Sweden
October 1990

(*Upper left*) Sarah Rice (Johanna) and Victor Garber (Anthony) and (*from lower left*) Joaquin Romaguera (Pirelli), Len Cariou (Sweeney Todd), Angela Lansbury (Mrs.

10

Lovett), Jack Eric Williams (the Beadle) and Edmund Lyndeck (Judge Turpin) in the original Broadway production of *Sweeney Todd, the Demon Barber of Fleet Street*

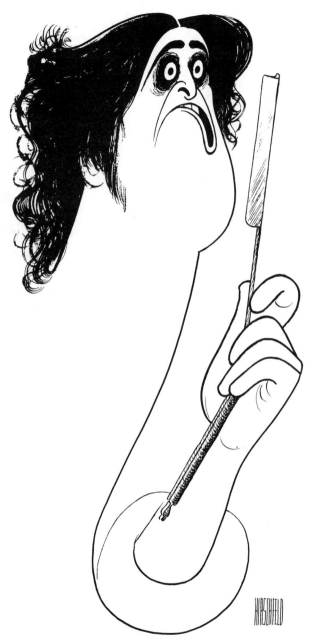

Len Cariou

Angela Lansbury

(*Lower left*) Jim Walton (Anthony) and Gretchen Kingsley (Johanna) and (*from upper left*) Michael McCarty (the Beadle), Bill Nabel (Pirelli), Bob Gunton (Sweeney Todd), David Baron (Judge Turpin), Beth Fowler (Mrs. Lovett) and Eddie Korbich (Tobias) in the 1989 Circle-in-the-Square revival of *Sweeney Todd*

15

Bob Gunton

Sweeney Todd

Todd

The Demon Barber of Fleet Street

To Flora and Janet Roberts

CAST OF CHARACTERS

ANTHONY HOPE

SWEENEY TODD

BEGGAR WOMAN

MRS. LOVETT

JUDGE TURPIN

THE BEADLE

JOHANNA

TOBIAS RAGG

PIRELLI

JONAS FOGG

TOWNSPEOPLE, LORDS, LADIES,
   POLICEMEN, LUNATICS, ETC.

Dorothy Loudon, who replaced Angela
Lansbury in the role of Mrs. Lovett

MUSICAL NUMBERS

ACT I

"The Ballad of Sweeney Todd"	COMPANY
"No Place Like London"	ANTHONY, TODD, BEGGAR WOMAN
"The Barber and His Wife"	TODD
"The Worst Pies in London"	MRS. LOVETT
"Poor Thing"	MRS. LOVETT
"My Friends"	TODD, MRS. LOVETT
"Green Finch and Linnet Bird"	JOHANNA
"Ah, Miss"	ANTHONY, BEGGAR WOMAN
"Johanna"	ANTHONY
"Pirelli's Miracle Elixir"	TOBIAS, TODD, MRS. LOVETT, COMPANY
"The Contest"	PIRELLI
"Johanna"	JUDGE TURPIN
"Wait"	MRS. LOVETT
"Kiss Me"	JOHANNA, ANTHONY
"Ladies in Their Sensitivities"	THE BEADLE
"Kiss Me"	JOHANNA, ANTHONY, THE BEADLE, JUDGE TURPIN
"Pretty Women"	TODD, JUDGE TURPIN
"Epiphany"	TODD
"A Little Priest"	TODD, MRS. LOVETT

ACT II

"God, That's Good!"	TOBIAS, MRS. LOVETT, TODD, BEGGAR WOMAN, CUSTOMERS
"Johanna"	ANTHONY, TODD, JOHANNA, BEGGAR WOMAN
"By the Sea"	MRS. LOVETT
Wigmaker Sequence	TODD, ANTHONY, QUINTET
"The Letter"	TODD, QUINTET
"Not While I'm Around"	TOBIAS, MRS. LOVETT
"Parlor Songs"	THE BEADLE, MRS. LOVETT, TOBIAS
"City on Fire"	LUNATICS, JOHANNA, ANTHONY
"Searching"	MRS. LOVETT, TODD, BEGGAR WOMAN, ANTHONY, JOHANNA
Final Sequence	MRS. LOVETT, TODD, BEGGAR WOMAN, JUDGE TURPIN
"The Ballad of Sweeney Todd"	COMPANY

Time: The 19th Century
Place: London: Fleet Street and environs

Prologue

As the audience enters, an organist takes his place at a huge eccentric organ to the side of the stage and begins to play funeral music. Before a front drop depicting in a honeycombed beehive the class system of mid-19th century England two gravediggers appear, carrying shovels, and begin to dig a grave downstage center. As they dig they disappear six feet into the earth, leaving piles of dirt on the upstage side.

At curtain time a police warden appears, looks at his watch, hurrying them. Two workmen enter. They pull down the drop. The deafeningly shrill sound of a factory whistle. Blackout.

The lights come up to reveal the company. A man steps forward and sings.

MAN:
Attend the tale of Sweeney Todd.
His skin was pale and his eye was odd.
He shaved the faces of gentlemen
Who never thereafter were heard of again.
He trod a path that few have trod,
Did Sweeney Todd,
The Demon Barber of Fleet Street.

ANOTHER MAN:

He kept a shop in London town,
Of fancy clients and good renown.
And what if none of their souls were saved?
They went to their maker impeccably shaved
By Sweeney,
By Sweeney Todd,
The Demon Barber of Fleet Street.

> (*A blinding light cuts down the stage as an upstage iron door opens. Two men enter. They carry a body in a bag, tied at both ends with rope. They are followed by a woman carrying a tin canister marked "Flour." They walk to the edge of the grave and unceremoniously dump the body in it. The woman opens the canister and pours black ashes into the hole. This action covers the next verse of the song*)

COMPANY:

Swing your razor wide, Sweeney!
Hold it to the skies!
Freely flows the blood of those
Who moralize!

> (*Various members of the company step forward and sing*)

SOLOISTS:

His needs were few, his room was bare:
A lavabo and a fancy chair,
A mug of suds and a leather strop,
An apron, a towel, a pail and a mop.
For neatness he deserves a nod,
Does Sweeney Todd,

COMPANY:

The Demon Barber of Fleet Street.

WOMEN:

Inconspicuous Sweeney was,
Quick and quiet and clean 'e was.

Back of his smile, under his word,
Sweeney heard music that nobody heard.
Sweeney pondered and Sweeney planned,
Like a perfect machine 'e planned.
Sweeney was smooth, Sweeney was subtle,
Sweeney would blink and rats would scuttle.

(*The men join in singing, voices overlapping, in a gradual crescendo*)

Sweeney was smooth, Sweeney was subtle,
Sweeney would blink and rats would scuttle.
Inconspicuous Sweeney was,
Quick and quiet and clean 'e was,
Like a perfect machine 'e was,
Was Sweeney!
Sweeney!
Sweeney!
Sweeeeeneeeeey!

(TODD *rises out of the grave and sings as the company repeats his words*)

TODD *and* COMPANY:

Attend the tale of Sweeney Todd.
He served a dark and a vengeful god.

TODD:

What happened then — well, that's the play,
And he wouldn't want us to give it away,
Not Sweeney,

TODD *and* COMPANY:

Not Sweeney Todd,
The Demon Barber of Fleet Street . . .

(*The scene blacks out. The bells of a clock tower chime. Early morning light comes up . . .*)

ACT I

A street by the London docks. A small boat appears from the back. In it are SWEENEY TODD, ANTHONY HOPE *and the pilot.* ANTHONY *is a cheerful country-born young ship's first mate with a duffel bag slung over his shoulder.* TODD *is a heavy-set, saturnine man in his forties who might, say, be a blacksmith or a dockhand. There is about him an air of brooding, slightly nerve-chilling self-absorption.*

ANTHONY (*Sings*):
I have sailed the world, beheld its wonders
From the Dardanelles
To the mountains of Peru,
But there's no place like London!
I feel home again.

I could hear the city bells
Ring whatever I would do.
No, there's no pl —

TODD (*Sings grimly*):
No, there's no place like London.

ANTHONY (*Surprised at the interruption*): Mr. Todd, sir?

TODD (*Sings*):
You are young.
Life has been kind to you.
You will learn.

29

(They step out of the boat, music under)
It is here we go our several ways. Farewell, Anthony, I will not soon forget the good ship *Bountiful* nor the young man who saved my life.

ANTHONY: There's no cause to thank me for that, sir. It would have been a poor Christian indeed who'd have spotted you pitching and tossing on that raft and not given the alarm.

TODD: There's many a Christian would have done just that and not lost a wink's sleep for it, either.
(A ragged BEGGAR WOMAN *suddenly appears)*

BEGGAR WOMAN *(Approaching, holding out bowl to* ANTHONY, *sings)*:
Alms! . . . Alms! . . .
For a miserable woman
On a miserable chilly morning . . .
       *(*ANTHONY *drops a coin in her bowl)*
Thank yer, sir, thank yer.
       (Softly, suddenly leering in a mad way)
'Ow would you like a little squiff, dear,
A little jig jig,
A little bounce around the bush?
Wouldn't you like to push me crumpet?
It looks to me, dear,
Like you got plenty there to push.
      (She grabs at him. As ANTHONY *starts back in embarrassment, she turns instantly and pathetically to* TODD, *who tries to keep his back to her)*
Alms! . . . Alms! . . .
For a pitiful woman
Wot's got wanderin' wits . . .
Hey, don't I know you, mister?
      (She peers intently at him)

TODD: Must you glare at me, woman? Off with you, off, I say!

BEGGAR WOMAN (*Smiling vacantly*):
Then 'ow would you like to fish me squiff, mister?
We'll go jig jig,
A little —

TODD (*Making a gesture as if to strike her*): Off, I said. To the devil with you!
(*She scuttles away, turns to give him a piercing look, then wanders off*)

BEGGAR WOMAN (*Singing as she goes*):
Alms! . . . Alms! . . .
For a desperate woman . . .
(*Music continues under*)

ANTHONY (*A little bewildered*): Pardon me, sir, but there's no need to fear the likes of her. She was only a half-crazed beggar woman. London's full of them.

TODD (*Half to himself, half to* ANTHONY): I beg your indulgence, boy. My mind is far from easy, for in these once-familiar streets I feel the chill of ghostly shadows everywhere. Forgive me.

ANTHONY: There's nothing to forgive.

TODD: Farewell, Anthony.

ANTHONY: Mr. Todd, before we part —

TODD (*Suddenly fierce*): What is it?

ANTHONY: I have honored my promise never to question you. Whatever brought you to that sorry shipwreck is your affair. And yet, during those many weeks of the voyage home, I have come to think of you as a friend and, if trouble lies ahead for you in London . . . if you need help — or money . . .

TODD (*Almost shouting*): No!

31

(ANTHONY *starts, perplexed;* TODD *makes a placating ges-*
ture, sings quietly and intensely)
There's a hole in the world
Like a great black pit
And the vermin of the world
Inhabit it
And its morals aren't worth
What a pig could spit
And it goes by the name of London.

At the top of the hole
Sit the privileged few,
Making mock of the vermin
In the lower zoo,
Turning beauty into filth and greed.
I too
Have sailed the world and seen its wonders,
For the cruelty of men
Is as wondrous as Peru,
But there's no place like London!
        (*Pause, music under, then as if in a trance*)
There was a barber and his wife,
And she was beautiful.
A foolish barber and his wife.
She was his reason and his life,
And she was beautiful.
And she was virtuous.
And he was —
                (*Shrugs*)
Naive.

There was another man who saw
That she was beautiful,
A pious vulture of the law
Who with a gesture of his claw
Removed the barber from his plate.

Then there was nothing but to wait
And she would fall,
So soft,
So young,
So lost,
And oh, so beautiful!
(*Pauses, music under*)

ANTHONY: And the lady, sir — did she — succumb?

TODD:
Oh, that was many years ago . . .
I doubt if anyone would know.
(*Speaks, music under*)
Now, leave me, Anthony, I beg of you. There's somewhere
I must go, something I must find out. Now. And alone.

ANTHONY: But surely we will meet again before I'm off to
Plymouth!

TODD: If you want, you may well find me. Around Fleet
Street, I wouldn't wonder.

ANTHONY: Well, until then, Mr. Todd.
(ANTHONY *starts off down the street.* TODD *stands a mo-*
ment alone in thought, then starts down the street in the
opposite direction)

TODD (*Sings*):
There's a hole in the world
Like a great black pit
And it's filled with people
Who are filled with shit
And the vermin of the world
Inhabit it . . .

(*As* TODD *disappears, we see* MRS. LOVETT'*s pieshop. Above*
it is any empty apartment which is reached by an outside
staircase. MRS. LOVETT, *a vigorous, slatternly woman in*

33

her forties, is flicking flies off the trays of pies with a dirty rag as she sings or hums. TODD *appears at the end of the street and moves slowly toward the pieshop, looking around as if remembering. Seeing the pieshop he pauses a moment at some distance, gazing at it and at* MRS. LOVETT, *who has now picked up a wicked-looking knife and starts chopping suet. After a beat,* TODD *moves toward the shop, hesitates and then enters.* MRS. LOVETT *does not notice him until his shadow passes across her. She looks up, knife in air, and screams, freezing him in his tracks)*

MRS. LOVETT: A customer!

> (TODD *has started out in alarm.* MRS. LOVETT *sings)*

Wait! What's yer rush? What's yer hurry?

> (*She sticks the knife into the counter)*

You gave me such a —

> (*She wipes her hands on her apron)*

Fright. I thought you was a ghost.
Half a minute, can'tcher?
Sit! Sit ye down!

> (*Forcing him into a chair)*

Sit!
All I meant is that I
Haven't seen a customer for weeks.
Did you come here for a pie, sir?

> (TODD *nods. She flicks a bit of dust off a pie with her rag)*

Do forgive me if me head's a little vague —
Ugh!

> (*She plucks something off a pie, holds it up)*

What is *that?*
But you'd think we had the plague —

> (*She drops it on the floor and stamps on it)*

From the way that people —

> (*She flicks something off a pie with her finger)*

Keep avoiding —

> (*Spotting it moving)*

34

No you don't!
>   (*She smacks it with her hand*)
Heaven knows I try, sir!
>   (*Lifts her hand, looks at it*)
Ick!
>   (*She wipes it on the edge of the counter*)
But there's no one comes in even to inhale —
Tsk!
>   (*She blows the last dust off the pie as she brings it to him*)
Right you are, sir. Would you like a drop of ale?
>   (TODD *nods*)
Mind you, I can't hardly blame them —
>   (*Pouring a tankard of ale*)
These are probably the worst pies in London.
I know why nobody cares to take them —
I *should* know,
I make them.
But good? No,
The worst pies in London —
Even that's polite.
The worst pies in London —
If you doubt it, take a bite.
>   (*He does*)
Is that just disgusting?
You have to concede it.
It's nothing but crusting —
Here, drink this, you'll need it —
>   (*She puts the ale in front of him*)
The worst pies in London —
>   (*During the following, she slams lumps of dough on the
>   counter and rolls them out, grunting frequently as she
>   goes*)
And no wonder with the price of meat
What it is
>   (*Grunt*)

35

When you get it.
> (*Grunt*)

Never
> (*Grunt*)

Thought I'd live to see the day men'd think it was a treat
Finding poor
> (*Grunt*)

Animals
> (*Grunt*)

Wot are dying in the street.
Mrs. Mooney has a pie shop,
Does a business, but I notice something weird —
Lately all her neighbors' cats have disappeared.
> (*Shrugs*)

Have to hand it to her —
Wot I calls
Enterprise,
Popping pussies into pies.
Wouldn't do in my shop —
Just the thought of it's enough to make you sick.
And I'm telling you them pussy cats is quick.
No denying times is hard, sir —
Even harder than
The worst pies in London.
Only lard and nothing more —
> (*As* TODD *gamely tries another mouthful*)

Is that just revolting?
All greasy and gritty,
It looks like it's molting,
And tastes like —
Well, pity
A woman alone
With limited wind
And the worst pies in London!
> (*Sighs heavily*)

Ah sir,
Times is hard. Times is hard.
>   (*She finishes one of the crusts with a flourish, then notices*
>   TODD *having difficulty with his pie, speaks*)

Spit it out, dear. Go on. On the floor. There's worse things
than that down there.
>   (*As he does*)

That's my boy.

TODD: Isn't that a room up there over the shop? If times are
so hard, why don't you rent it out? That should bring in
something.

MRS. LOVETT: Up there? Oh, no one will go near it. People
think it's haunted. You see — years ago, something happened up there. Something not very nice.
>   (*Sings*)

There was a barber and his wife,
And he was beautiful,
A proper artist with a knife,
But they transported him for life.
>   (*Sighs*)

And he was beautiful . . .
>   (*Speaks, music continuing under*)

Barker, his name was — Benjamin Barker.

TODD: Transported? What was his crime?

MRS. LOVETT: Foolishness.
>   (*Sings*)

He had this wife, you see,
Pretty little thing.
Silly little nit
Had her chance for the moon on a string —
Poor thing. Poor thing.
>   (*As she sings, her narration is acted out. First we see the pret-*
>   *ty young* WIFE *in the empty upstairs room dancing her house-*
>   *hold chores. During the following the* JUDGE *and his obse-*

quious assistant, the BEADLE, *approach the house, gazing up at the* WIFE *lecherously. The* WIFE *remains demure, sewing*)

There were these two, you see,
Wanted her like mad,
One of 'em a Judge,
T'other one his Beadle.
Every day they'd nudge
And they'd wheedle.
But she wouldn't budge
From her needle.
Too bad. Pure thing.

(*Far upstage, in very dim light, shapes appear. A swirl of cloth, glints of jewels, the faces of people masked as animals and demons. During the following lyric, the* WIFE *takes an imaginary baby from an imaginary cot and sits on the floor, cradling it in her arms as she sobs*)

So they merely shipped the poor bugger off south,
    they did,
Leaving her with nothing but grief and a year-old kid.
Did she use her head even then? Oh no, God forbid!
Poor fool.
Ah, but there was worse yet to come —
                    (*Intake of breath*)
Poor thing.

(*Again the shapes appear, this time a bit more distinctly.* MRS. LOVETT *speaks, musingly*)

Johanna, that was the baby's name . . . Pretty little Johanna . . .
            (*Drifts off in reminiscence*)

TODD (*Tensely*): Go on.

MRS. LOVETT (*Eyeing* TODD *sharply*): My, you do like a good story, don't you?
    (*The* BEADLE *reappears, gazing up at the* WIFE, *miming in a solicitous manner for her to come down.* MRS. LOVETT, *warming to the tale, sings*)

Well, Beadle calls on her, all polite,
Poor thing, poor thing.
The Judge, he tells her, is all contrite,
He blames himself for her dreadful plight,
She must come straight to his house tonight!
Poor thing, poor thing.
                    (*Excited, almost gleeful*)
Of course, when she goes there,
Poor thing, poor thing.
They're havin' this ball all in masks.
    (*The shapes are now clear. A ball is in progress at the
    JUDGE's house: the company, wearing grotesque masks, is
    dancing a slow minuet. The BEADLE, leading the WIFE,
    appears, moving with her through the dancers. He gives
    her champagne. She looks dazedly around, terrified*)
There's no one she knows there,
Poor dear, poor thing.
She wanders tormented, and drinks,
Poor thing.
The Judge has repented, she thinks,
Poor thing.
"Oh, where is Judge Turpin?" she asks.
    (*During the following, the JUDGE appears, tears off his
    mask, then his cloak, revealing himself naked. The WIFE
    screams as he reaches for her, struggling wildly as the BEA-
    DLE hurls her to the floor. He holds her there as the JUDGE
    mounts her and the masked dancers pirouette around the
    ravishment, giggling*)
He was there, all right —
Only not so contrite!
She wasn't no match for such craft, you see,
And everyone thought it so droll.
They figured she had to be daft, you see,
So all of 'em stood there and laughed, you see.
Poor soul!
Poor thing!

TODD (*A wild shout*): Would no one have mercy on her?
(*The dumb show vanishes. Music stops.* TODD *and* MRS. LOVETT *gaze at each other*)

MRS. LOVETT (*Coolly*): So it is you — Benjamin Barker.

TODD (*Frighteningly vehement*): Not Barker! Not Barker! Todd now! Sweeney Todd! Where is she?

MRS. LOVETT: So changed! Good God, what did they do to you down there in bloody Australia or wherever?

TODD: Where is my wife? Where's Lucy?

MRS. LOVETT: She poisoned herself. Arsenic from the apothecary on the corner. I tried to stop her but she wouldn't listen to me.

TODD: And my daughter?

MRS. LOVETT: Johanna? He's got her.

TODD: He? Judge Turpin?

MRS. LOVETT: Even he had a conscience tucked away, I suppose. Adopted her like his own. You could say it was good luck for her . . . almost.

TODD: Fifteen years sweating in a living hell on a trumped up charge. Fifteen years dreaming that, perhaps, I might come home to a loving wife and child.
(*Strikes ferociously on the pie counter with his fists*)
Let them quake in their boots — Judge Turpin and the Beadle — for their hour has come.

MRS. LOVETT (*Awed*): You're going to — get 'em? You? A bleeding little nobody of a runaway convict? Don't make me laugh. You'll never get His 'igh and Mightiness! Nor the Beadle neither. Not in a million years.
(*No reaction from* TODD)
You got any money?

(*Still no reaction*)
Listen to me! You got any money?

TODD: No money.

MRS. LOVETT: Then how you going to live even?

TODD: I'll live. If I have to sweat in the sewers or in the plague hospital, I'll live — and I'll have them.

MRS. LOVETT: Oh, you poor thing! You poor thing!
(*A sudden thought*)
Wait!
(*She disappears behind a curtained entrance leading to her parlor. For a beat* TODD *stands alone, almost exalted.* MRS. LOVETT *returns with a razor case. She holds it out to him*)
See! It don't have to be the sewers or the plague hospital. When they come for the little girl, I hid 'em. I thought, who knows? Maybe the poor silly blighter'll be back again someday and need 'em. Cracked in the head, wasn't I? Times as bad as they are, I could have got five, maybe ten quid for 'em, any day. See? You can be a barber again.
(*Music begins. She opens the case for him to look inside.*
TODD *stands a long moment gazing down at the case*)
My, them handles is chased silver, ain't they?

TODD: Silver, yes.
(*Quietly, looking into the box, sings*)
These are my friends.
See how they glisten.
(*Picks up a small razor*)
See this one shine,
How he smiles in the light.
My friend, my faithful friend.
(*Holding it to his ear, feeling the edge with his thumb*)
Speak to me, friend.
Whisper, I'll listen.
(*Listening*)

41

I know, I know —
You've been locked out of sight
All these years —
Like me, my friend.
Well, I've come home
To find you waiting.
Home,
And we're together,
And we'll do wonders,
Won't we?

> (MRS. LOVETT, *who has been looking over his shoulder,*
> *starts to feel his other ear lightly, absently, in her own*
> *trance.* TODD *lays the razor back in the box and picks out a*
> *larger one. They sing simultaneously*)

TODD:
You there, my friend.
Come, let me hold you.

MRS. LOVETT:
I'm your friend too, Mr. Todd.
If you only knew, Mr. Todd —

Now, with a sigh
You grow warm
In my hand,
My friend,
My clever friend.
(*Putting it back*)
Rest now, my friends.
Soon I'll unfold you.
Soon you'll know splendors

Ooh, Mr. Todd,
You're warm
In my hand.
You've come home.
Always had a fondness for you,
I did.

Never you fear, Mr. Todd,
You can move in here,
    Mr. Todd.

You never have dreamed

Splendors you never have
    dreamed

All your days,
My lucky friends.
Till now your shine
Was merely silver.
Friends,

All your days
Will be yours.
I'm your friend.
Don't they shine beautiful?
Silver's good enough for me,

42

You shall drip rubies,   Mr. T. . . .
You'll soon drip precious
Rubies . . .

> (TODD *holds up the biggest razor to the light as the music soars sweetly, then stops. He speaks into the silence*)

TODD: My right arm is complete again!

> (*Lights dim except for a scalding spot on the razor as music blares forth from both the organ and the orchestra. The company, including the* JUDGE *and the* BEADLE, *appears and sings*)

COMPANY:
Lift your razor high, Sweeney!
Hear it singing, "Yes!"
Sink it in the rosy skin
Of righteousness!

> (*Variously*)

His voice was soft, his manner mild.
He seldom laughed but he often smiled.
He'd seen how civilized men behave.
He never forgot and he never forgave,
Not Sweeney,
Not Sweeney Todd,
The Demon Barber of Fleet Street . . .

> (*They disappear. There is a moment of darkness in which we hear the trilling and twittering of songbirds. Light comes up on the facade of* JUDGE TURPIN*'s mansion. A* BIRD SELLER *enters carrying a bizarre construction of little wicker birdcages tied together. It is in these that the birds are singing. At an upper level of the* JUDGE*'s mansion appears a very young, exquisitely beautiful girl with a long mane of shining blonde hair. This is* JOHANNA. *For a moment she stands disconsolate, then her eyes fall on the birds*)

JOHANNA: And how are they today?

BIRD SELLER: Hungry as always, Miss Johanna.
               (*He lifts the cages up to her*)

JOHANNA (*Sings*):
    Green finch and linnet bird,
    Nightingale, blackbird,
    How is it you sing?
    How can you jubilate,
    Sitting in cages,
    Never taking wing?
    Outside the sky waits,
    Beckoning, beckoning,
    Just beyond the bars.
    How can you remain,
    Staring at the rain,
    Maddened by the stars?
    How is it you sing
    Anything?
    How is it you sing?

    Green finch and linnet bird,
    Nightingale, blackbird,
    How is it you sing?
    Whence comes this melody constantly flowing?
    Is it rejoicing or merely halloing?
    Are you discussing or fussing
    Or simply dreaming?
    Are you crowing?
    Are you screaming?

    Ringdove and robinet,
    Is it for wages,
    Singing to be sold?
    Have you decided it's
    Safer in cages,
    Singing when you're told?

44

(ANTHONY *enters. Instantly he sees her and stands transfixed by her beauty*)
My cage has many rooms,
Damask and dark.
Nothing there sings,
Not even my lark.
Larks never will, you know,
When they're captive.
Teach me to be more adaptive.

Green finch and linnet bird,
Nightingale, blackbird,
Teach me how to sing.
If I cannot fly,
Let me sing.
                (*She gazes into the middle distance disconsolately*)

ANTHONY (*Gazing at her, sings softly*):
I have sailed the world,
Beheld its wonders,
From the pearls of Spain
To the rubies of Tibet,
But not even in London
Have I seen such a wonder . . .
                (*Breathlessly*)
Lady look at me look at me miss oh
Look at me please oh
Favor me favor me with your glance.
Ah, miss,
What do you what do you see off
There in those trees oh
Won't you give won't you give me a chance?

Who would sail to Spain
For all its wonders,
When in Kearney's Lane

Lies the greatest wonder yet?

Ah, miss,
Look at you look at you pale and
Ivory-skinned oh
Look at you looking so sad so queer.
Promise
Not to retreat to the darkness
Back of your window
Not till you not till you look down here.
Look at

ANTHONY:	JOHANNA:
Me!	Green finch and linnet bird,
Look at	Nightingale, blackbird,
Me!	Teach me how to sing.
	If I cannot fly,
Look at me . . .	Let me sing . . .

> (*As* JOHANNA *turns back to go inside, their eyes meet and the song dies on their lips. A hushed moment. Then suddenly a clawlike hand darts out from a pile of trash.* ANTHONY *jumps and looks down to see the* BEGGAR WOMAN, *who has been sleeping in the garbage under a discarded shawl, thrusting her bowl at him.* JOHANNA, *frightened, slips back out of sight*)

BEGGAR WOMAN (*Sings*):
Alms! . . . Alms! . . .
For a miserable woman . . .
> (ANTHONY *hurriedly digs out a coin and drops it in her bowl; she peers at him*)
Beg your pardon, it's you, sir . . .
Thank yer . . . Thank yer kindly . . .
> (ANTHONY *turns back to discover* JOHANNA *gone and the window shut. The* BEGGAR WOMAN *starts off*)

ANTHONY: One moment, mother.
> (*She turns*)

Perhaps you know whose house this is?

BEGGAR WOMAN: That! That's the great Judge Turpin's house, that is.

ANTHONY: And the young lady who resides there?

BEGGAR WOMAN: Ah, her! That's Johanna, his pretty little ward.
     (Slyly confidential)
But don't you go trespassing there, young man. Not if you value your hide.
     (She nods her head)
Tamper there and it's a good whipping for you — or any other youth with mischief on his mind.
     (Leers at him, sings)
Hey! Hoy! Sailor boy!
Want it snugly harbored?
Open me gate, but dock it straight,
I see it lists to starboard.
  (She grabs at his crotch and starts to dance around him grotesquely, lifting her skirts. ANTHONY is appalled. He pulls coins out of his pocket and tosses them to her)

ANTHONY: Here and here and here. Take it and off with you. Off!
  (The BEGGAR WOMAN, cackling, collects the coins and scampers off. ANTHONY turns back to the house, gazes up at the window. The noise has frightened the birds, who start screeching. ANTHONY becomes aware of them and moves over to the now sleeping BIRD SELLER, shakes him awake, and inspects the cages. Music continues under)
Which one sings the sweetest?

BIRD SELLER: All's the same, sir. Six pence and cheap at the price.
  (ANTHONY selects one, gives the man a coin, holds up the cage)

47

ANTHONY: He sings bravely.
> (*Watches the cage*)

But why does he batter his wings so wildly against the bars?

BIRD SELLER: We blind 'em, sir. That's what we always does. Blind 'em and, not knowing night from day, they sing and sing without stopping, pretty creatures.
> (*He gets up, slinging the cages on his back, and starts off*)

Have pleasure of the bird, sir.
> (*He exits.* JOHANNA *reappears at the window.* ANTHONY *holds up the cage, indicating it is a present and she should come down to get it. She hesitates, smiles, nods, disappears from the window. He waits. Shyly, almost furtively,* JOHANNA *slips out of the door and stands there. He moves toward her, holding out the cage. Slowly her hand goes out toward him. Their fingers touch*)

ANTHONY (*Sings softly*):
I feel you,
Johanna,
I feel you.
I was half convinced I'd waken,
Satisfied enough to dream you.
Happily I was mistaken,
Johanna!
I'll steal you,
Johanna,
I'll steal you . . .
> (*They stand so absorbed with each other that they do not notice the approach of* JUDGE TURPIN, *followed by the* BEADLE)

JUDGE (*Shouting*): Johanna! Johanna!

JOHANNA: Oh dear!
> (*Forgetting the bird cage,* JOHANNA *scurries toward the house.* ANTHONY *turns to find the* JUDGE *glaring at him*)

JUDGE: If I see your face again on this or any other neighbor street, you'll rue the day you were born. Is that plain enough speaking for you?

ANTHONY: But, sir, I swear to you there was nothing in my heart but the most respectful sentiments of —

JUDGE (*To* BEADLE): Dispose of him!
(*He strides toward the house*)

JOHANNA: Oh dear! I knew!

BEADLE (*Fondling the truncheon, to* ANTHONY): You heard His Worship.

ANTHONY: But, friend, I have no fight with you.
(*The* BEADLE *takes the cage from him, opens its door, takes out the bird, wrings its neck and then tosses it away*)

BEADLE: Get the gist of it, friend? Next time it'll be *your* neck!
(*He starts after the* JUDGE *and* JOHANNA)

JUDGE: Johanna, if I were to think you encouraged that young rogue . . .

JOHANNA: Oh father, I hope always to be obedient to your commands.

JUDGE (*Relenting, patting her cheek*): Dear child.
(*Gazing at her lustfully*)
How sweet you look in that light muslin gown.
(*She runs into the house, the* JUDGE *after her. The* BEADLE *follows.* ANTHONY *is left alone, the empty cage in his hand*)

ANTHONY (*Sings*):
I'll steal you,
Johanna,
I'll steal you!
Do they think that walls can hide you?

49

Even now I'm at your window.
I am in the dark beside you,
Buried sweetly in your yellow hair.

I feel you,
Johanna,
And one day
I'll steal you.
Till I'm with you then,
I'm with you there,
Sweetly buried in your yellow hair . . .
(*He smashes the cage, throws it away and exits as lights
fade*)

(*Lights come up to reveal St. Dunstan's Marketplace. A
hand-drawn caravan, painted like a Sicilian donkey cart,
stands on the street. On its side is written in ornate script:
"Signor Adolfo Pirelli — Haircutter-Barber-Toothpuller to
His Royal Majesty the King of Naples," and under this:
"Banish Baldness with Pirelli's Miracle Elixir."* TODD
and MRS. LOVETT *enter.* TODD *is carrying his razor case.*
MRS. LOVETT *has a shopping basket*)

TODD (*Pointing at the caravan*): That's him? Over there?

MRS. LOVETT: Yes, dear. He's always here Thursdays.

TODD (*Reading the sign*): Haircutter, barber, toothpuller to
His Royal Majesty the King of Naples.

MRS. LOVETT: Eyetalian. All the rage, he is.

TODD: Not for long.

MRS. LOVETT: Oh Mr. T., you really think you can do it?

TODD: By tomorrow they'll all be flocking after me like
sheep to be shorn.

MRS. LOVETT (*Sees* BEADLE): Oh no! Look. The Beadle —
Beadle Bamford.

TODD: So much the better.

MRS. LOVETT: But what if he recognizes you? Hadn't we better — ?

TODD: I will do what I have set out to do, woman.

MRS. LOVETT: Oops. Sorry, dear, I'm sure.
(TOBIAS, PIRELLI*'s adolescent, simple-minded assistant, appears through a curtain at the rear of the caravan, beating on a tin drum. A factory whistle blows and a crowd of people comes running on, gathering around him)*

TOBIAS (*Sings*):
Ladies and gentlemen!
May I have your attention, perlease?
Do you wake every morning in shame and despair
To discover your pillow is covered with hair
Wot ought not to be there?

Well, ladies and gentlemen,
From now on you can waken at ease.
You need never again have a worry or care,
I will show you a miracle marvelous rare.
Gentlemen, you are about to see something wot rose
   from the dead!
(*A woman gasps — he smiles and wiggles his finger no*)
On the top of my head.

Scarcely a month ago, gentlemen,
I was struck with a 'orrible
Dermatologic disease.
Though the finest physicians in London were called,
I awakened one morning amazed and appalled
To discover with dread that my head was as bald
As a novice's knees.
I was dying of shame
Till a gentleman came,

51

An illustrious barber, Pirelli by name.
He give me a liquid as precious as gold,
I rubbed it in daily like wot I was told,
And behold!
> (*Doffs his cap dramatically, revealing mountains of hair which cascade to his shoulders*)
Only thirty days old!

'Twas Pirelli's
Miracle Elixir,
That's wot did the trick, sir,
True, sir, true.
Was it quick, sir?
Did it in a tick, sir,
Just like an elixir
Ought to do!

> (*To* 1ST MAN)
How about a bottle, mister?
Only costs a penny, guaranteed.
> (*Crowd, overlapping*)

1ST MAN:
Penny buys a bottle, I don't know . . .

2ND MAN:
You don't need —

1ST MAN:
Ah, let's go!
> (*Starts to leave*)

TOBIAS (*To* 3RD MAN):
Go ahead and tug, sir.

3RD MAN:
Penny for a bottle, is it?

TOBIAS:
Go ahead, sir, harder . . .

TOBIAS (*Stopping the* 1ST MAN, *who's quite bald, by pouring a drop on his head*):
Does Pirelli's
Stimulate the growth, sir?
You can have my oath, sir,
'Tis unique.
> (*Takes the man's hand and gently applies it to the wet spot*)
Rub a minute.
Stimulatin', i'n' it?
Soon you'll have to thin it
Once a week!
Penny buys a bottle, guaranteed!
> (*Crowd, overlapping*)

1ST MAN (*To* 2ND MAN):
Penny buys a bottle, might as well . . .
> (*Looks hesitantly to* 2ND MAN)

3RD MAN:
Wotcher think?

2ND WOMAN:
Go ahead and try it, wot the hell . . .

TOBIAS (*To others*):
How about a sample? Have you ever smelled a cleaner smell?

1ST WOMAN (*To* 3RD MAN):
Isn't it a crime they let these urchins clog the pavement?

4TH MAN:
Penny buys a bottle, does it?

TOBIAS (*To* 2ND MAN):
That's enough, sir, ample.

TOBIAS:
Gently dab it.

Gets to be a habit.
Soon there'll be enough, sir,
Somebody can grab it.
                    (*Points to a man standing nearby*)
See that chap with
Hair like Shelley's?
You can tell 'e's
Used Pirelli's!
                    (*Crowd, overlapping*)

1ST MAN:
    Let me have a bottle.

2ND MAN:
    Make that two.
                    (1ST MAN *buys bottles for both, gets change*)

3RD WOMAN:
    Come to think of it, I could get some for Harry . . .

4TH WOMAN:
    Nothing works on Harry, dear. Bye bye.

TOBIAS:
    Go ahead and feel, mum.
    Absolutely real, mum . . .

2ND MAN (*To* 1ST MAN):
    How about a beer?

1ST MAN:
    You know a pub?

2ND MAN:
    There's one close by.

1ST WOMAN (*To* 2ND WOMAN):
    You got all the hair you need now.

3RD MAN:
    That's no lie.

54

4TH MAN:
  Pass it by.

2ND WOMAN:
  I'm just passing by.

TODD (*Loudly to* MRS. LOVETT):
  Pardon me, ma'am, what's that awful stench?

MRS. LOVETT:
  Are we standing in an open trench?

TODD:
  Must be standing near an open trench!

TOBIAS (*Distracting the crowd's attention*):
  Buy Pirelli's Miracle Elixir:
  Anything wot's slick, sir,
  Soon sprouts curls.
  Try Pirelli's!
  When they see how thick, sir,
  You can have your pick, sir,
  Of the girls!
                (*To* 4TH WOMAN)
  Want to buy a bottle, missus?
                (*Crowd, overlapping*)

TODD (*Sniffing* 1ST MAN's *bottle*):
  What is this?

MRS. LOVETT (*Examining* 3RD MAN's *bottle*):
  What is this?

1ST MAN:
  Propogates the hair, sir.

4TH MAN:
  I'll take one!

TODD (*Hands bottle back distastefully*):
  Smells like piss.

MRS. LOVETT:
   Smells like — phew!

2ND MAN:
   He says it smells like piss.

TODD:
   Looks like piss.

MRS. LOVETT:
   Wouldn't touch it if I was you, dear!

2ND MAN (*To* 3RD MAN):
   Wotcher think?

TODD (*Nods*):
   This is piss. Piss with ink.

5TH MAN *and* WOMEN:
   Says it smells like piss or something.

TOBIAS:
   Penny for a bottle . . .
   Have you ever smelled a cleaner smell?
   How about a sample? . . .
   How about a sample, mister? . . .

1ST WOMAN:
   Give us back our money!

2ND WOMAN:
   Give us back our money!

1ST WOMAN:
   Did you ever — ?
   Give us back our money!

3RD WOMAN:
   Glad I didn't buy one, I can tell you!

4TH WOMAN (*To* TOBIAS):
   If you think that piss can fool a lady, you're mistaken!

MRS. LOVETT:

Give 'em back their money!
Did you ever — ?
Give 'em back their money!

3RD WOMAN:

Give 'em back their money, I say!
Give 'em back their money!

TOBIAS (*Trying to calm them, gesturing to* TODD):

Never mind that madman, mister . . .
Never mind the madman . . .

TODD *and* MRS. LOVETT:

Where is this Pirelli?

CROWD:

Where is this Pirelli?
                   (*Variously, overlapping*)
What about my money, laddie?
Yes, what about the money?
Hand it back!
We don't want no piss, boy!
Give it here . . .

TOBIAS (*Desperately, beating the drum out of rhythm*):

Let Pirelli's
Activate your roots, sir —

TODD:

Keep it off your boots, sir —
Eats right through.

CROWD:

Go and get Pirelli!

TOBIAS:

Yes, get Pirelli's!
Use a bottle of it!
Ladies seem to love it —

57

MRS. LOVETT:

Flies do, too!

(*Crowd laughs uproariously*)

CROWD:

Hand the bloody money over!
Hand the bloody money over!

TOBIAS (*Frenetically fast, looking desperately toward the curtain*):

See Pirelli's
Miracle Elixir
Grow a little wick, sir,
Then some fuzz.
The Pirelli's
Soon'll make it thick, sir,
Like a good elixir
Always does!

Trust Pirelli's!
If your hair is sick, sir,
Fix it in the nick, sir,
Don't look grim.
Just Pirelli's
Miracle Elixir,
That'll do the trick, sir —

1ST MAN:

What about the money?

TOBIAS:

If you've got a kick, sir —

CROWD (*Individuals, building to a shout*):

What about the money?
Where is this Pirelli?
Go and get Pirelli!
What about our money?

TOBIAS:

Tell it to the mixer

Of the Miracle Elixir —
If you've got a kick, sir — !
>(*Desperately yanks the curtain aside, revealing* PIRELLI, *an excessively flamboyant Italian with a glittering suit, thick wavy hair and a dazzling smile — the crowd falls silent, stunned.* TOBIAS *collapses, exhausted*)

Talk to him!

PIRELLI (*Bows and poses splendidly for a moment, in one hand an ornate razor, in the other a sinister-looking tooth-extractor; sings*):
I am Adolfo Pirelli,
Da king of da barbers, da barber of kings,
E buon giorno, good day,
I blow you a kiss!
>(*He does*)

And I, da so-famous Pirelli,
I wish-a to know-a
Who has-a da nerve-a to say
My elixir is piss!
Who says this?

TODD: I do.
>(*He holds up the bottle of elixir*)

I am Mr. Sweeney Todd and I have opened a bottle of Pirelli's Elixir, and I say to you it is nothing but an arrant fraud, concocted from piss and ink.
>(MRS. LOVETT *takes the bottle from* TODD, *sniffs it*)

MRS. LOVETT: He's right. Phew! Better to throw your money down the sewer.
>(*She tosses the bottle to the ground. The onlookers "ooh" and "aah" with shocked excitement*)

TOBIAS (*Beating agitatedly on the drum, shouting*): Ladies and gentlemen, pay no attention to that madman. Who's to be the first for a magnificent shave?

TODD (*Breaking in*): And furthermore . . .

(*Glaring at* PIRELLI)

I have serviced no kings, yet I wager that I can shave a cheek and pull a tooth with ten times more dexterity than any street mountebank!

(*He holds up his razor case for the crowd to see*)
You see these razors?

MRS. LOVETT: The finest in England.

TODD (*To* PIRELLI): I lay them against five pounds you are no match for me. You hear me, sir? Either accept my challenge or reveal yourself as a sham.

MRS. LOVETT: Bravo, bravo.

(*The crowd laughs and cheers, obviously on* TODD*'s side.*
PIRELLI, *as imposing as ever, holds up a hand for silence.*
Slowly he swaggers toward TODD, *takes the razor case,*
opens it and examines the razors carefully)

PIRELLI (*He speaks with a fairly obvious put-on foreign accent,*
barely concealing an Irish underlay): Zees are indeed fine razors. Instruments like zees once seen cannot be soon forgotten.

(*Takes out a tooth-extractor*)
And a fine extractor, too! You wager zees against five pounds, sir?

TODD: I do.

PIRELLI (*Addressing the crowd*): You hear zis foolish man? Watch and see how he will regret his folly. Five pounds it is!

(*Music starts*)

TODD (*Surveying the crowd*): Friends, neighbors, who's for a free shave?

1ST MAN (*Stepping forward eagerly*): Me, Mr. Todd, sir.

2ND MAN (*Stepping forward eagerly, too*): And me, Mr. Todd, sir.

TODD: Over here. Bring me a chair.

PIRELLI (*To* TOBIAS): Boy, bring ze basins, bring ze towels!

TOBIAS: Yes, sir . . .

PIRELLI: Quick!
(*He kicks* TOBIAS. *The boy hurries off into the caravan*)

TODD: Will Beadle Bamford be the judge?

BEADLE: Glad, as always, to oblige my friends and neighbors.
(*As another man comes on with a wooden chair and* TOBIAS *emerges from the caravan with basins, towels, etc., the* BEADLE *instantly takes over. To man, indicating where to set the chair*)
Put it there.
(1ST MAN *sits on* TODD*'s chair. The* 2ND MAN *is ensconced on* PIRELLI*'s chair.* PIRELLI *shakes out a fancy bib with a flourish and covers his man.* TODD *takes a towel and tucks it around his man's neck*)
Ready?

PIRELLI: Ready!

TODD: Ready!

BEADLE: The fastest, smoothest shave is the winner.
(*He blows his whistle. The music becomes agitated. The contest begins.* PIRELLI *strops his razor quickly,* TODD *in a leisurely manner.* PIRELLI *keeps glancing at* TODD *in various paranoid ways throughout, frightened of* TODD*'s progress. He starts whipping up lather rapidly*)

PIRELLI (*Sings to crowd while mixing, furiously*):
Now, signorini, signori,
We mix-a da lather
But first-a you gather
Around, signor-
Ini, signori,
You looking a man
Who have had-a da glory

To shave-a da Pope!
Mr. Sweeney-so-smart —
                    (*Sarcastic bow to* TODD)
Oh, I beg-a you pardon — 'll
Call me a lie, was-a only a cardinal —
Nope!
It was-a da Pope!
   (*Looks over shoulder, sees* TODD *still stropping slowly,
   gains confidence, starts to lather his man's face*)
Perhaps, signorini, signori,
You like-a I tell-a
Da famous-a story
Of Queen Isabella,
Da Queen of-a Polan'
Whose toot' was-a swollen,
I pull it so nice from her mout'
That-a though to begin
She's-a screaming-a murder,
She's later-a swoon-a wid
Bliss an' was heard-a
To shout:
"Pull all of 'em out!"
   (*Unexpectedly,* TODD *still shows no sign of starting to
   shave his man. He merely watches* PIRELLI*'s performance.*
   PIRELLI, *now feeling that he can take his time, sings lyri-
   cally as he shaves with rhythmic scrapes and elaborate ges-
   tures of wiping the razor*)
To shave-a da face,
To pull-a da toot',
Require da grace
And not-a da brute,
For if-a you slip,
You nick da skin,
You clip-a da chin,
You rip-a da lip a bit
And dat's-a da trut'!

(TODD *strops his razor slowly and deliberately, disconcert-ing* PIRELLI *and drawing the crowd's attention*)
To shave-a da face
Or even a part
Widout it-a smart
Require da heart.
It take-a da art —
I show you a chart —
(*Pulls down an elaborate chart with many anatomical views of the face and closeups of follicles, etc.*)
I study-a starting in my yout'!
(TODD *starts slowly mixing his lather*)
To cut-a da hair,
To trim-a da beard,
To make-a da bristle
Clean like a whistle,
Dis is from early infancy
Da talent give to me
By God!
It take-a da skill,
It take-a da brains,
It take-a da will
To take-a da pains,
It take-a da pace,
It take-a da grace —
(*While* PIRELLI *holds this note elaborately,* TODD, *with a few deft strokes, quickly lathers his man's face, shaves him and signals the* BEADLE *to examine the job*)

BEADLE (*Blowing whistle*):
The winner is Todd.

MRS. LOVETT (*Feeling the customer's cheek*): Smooth as a baby's arse!
(*The crowd "oohs" and "ahhs"*)

TODD (*Looks around*): And now, who's for a tooth pulling — free without charge!

MAN WITH HEAD TIED UP IN RAG: Me, sir. Me, sir.
>   (*He runs to the chair vacated by the shaved man*)

TODD (*Looking around*): Who else?
>   (*There is silence from the crowd*)
No one?
>   (*Turning to the* BEADLE)
Then, sir, since there is no means to test the second skill,
I claim the five pounds!

MRS. LOVETT: To which he is entitled!
>   (*To crowd*)
Right?
>   (*The crowd applauds*)

PIRELLI: Wait! One moment. Wait!
>   (*He turns to* TOBIAS)
You, boy. Get on that chair.

TOBIAS (*In terror*): Me, signor? Oh, not a tooth, sir, I beg of
you! I ain't got a twinge — not the tiniest pain. I —

PIRELLI (*Giving him a stinging blow on the cheek*): You do now!
>   (*Forces him into the chair. Turning to the crowd*)
We see who is zee victor now. Zis Mister Todd — or zee
great Pirelli!

BEADLE: Ready?

PIRELLI: Ready!

TODD: Ready!
>   (*The* BEADLE *blows his whistle. While* TODD, *even more
>   nonchalant than before, merely stands by his patient,*
>   PIRELLI *forces open the mouth of* TOBIAS, *brandishing his
>   extractor. He peers in, selects a tooth, thrusts the extractor
>   into the mouth and starts to tug while singing with pre-
>   tended ease. During the song,* TOBIAS *starts moaning, then
>   screaming — musically*)

PIRELLI (*Sings*):

To pull-a da toot'
Widout-a da skill
Can damage da root —
(As TOBIAS *squirms)*
Now hold-a da still!
An' if-a you slip
You grip a bit,
You hit da pit of it
Or chip-a da tip
And have-a to fill!

To pull-a da toot'
Widout-a da grace,
You leave-a da space
All over da place.
You try to erase
Widout-a da trace . . .
(Glaring archly at TODD)
Sometimes is da case
You even-a kill.
(TODD *still watches;* PIRELLI *is having trouble,* TOBIAS*'s wails are becoming louder*)
To hold-a da clamp
Widout-a da cramp,
Wid all dat saliva,
It could-a drive-a
You crazy — !
(To TOBIAS, *who is groaning)*
Don' mutter,
Or back-a you go to da gutter —
(To the crowd, forcing a smile)
My touch is as light as a butter-a
Cup!

I take-a da pains,

I learn-a da art,
I use-a da brains,
I give-a da heart,
I have-a da grace,
I win-a da race — !
> (*While again* PIRELLI *holds the note,* TODD *stands watching. Then in one swift move, he tugs the rag off his patient's head, neatly opens the mouth, looks in, and with a single deft motion of the extractor, gives a tiny tug and, turning to the crowd, holds up the extracted tooth. The* BEADLE *blows his whistle. The crowd roars its approval.* PIRELLI, *cut off again in the middle of his high note, sees that* TODD *has extracted his customer's tooth, and droops*)

I give-a da up.

MAN (*Jumping up from chair*): Not a twinge of pain! Not a twinge!

MRS. LOVETT: The man's a bloody marvel!

BEADLE (*Beaming at* TODD): The two-time winner — Mr. Sweeney Todd!
> (PIRELLI *leaves the tooth unpulled in* TOBIAS's *mouth and, still retaining his imposing dignity, moves over to* TODD)

PIRELLI (*With profound bow*): Sir, I bow to a skill far defter than my own.

TODD: The five pounds.

PIRELLI (*Produces a rather flamboyant purse, and from it takes five pounds*): Here, sir. And may the good Lord smile on you —
> (*With a sinister smile*)

— until we meet again. Come, boy.
> (*Bows to crowd*)

Signori! Bellissime signorini! Buon giorno! Buon giorno a tutti!
> (*Kicking* TOBIAS *ahead of him, he returns to the caravan which* TOBIAS, *like a horse, pulls off*)

MRS. LOVETT (*To* TODD): Who'd have thought it, dear! You pulled it off!

(*The crowd clusters around* TODD)

MAN WITH CAP: Oh, sir, Mr. Todd, sir, do you have an establishment of your own?

MRS. LOVETT: He certainly does. Sweeney Todd's Tonsorial Parlor — above my meat pieshop on Fleet Street.

(*The* BEADLE *strolls somewhat menacingly over to them*)

BEADLE: Mr. Todd . . . Strange, sir, but it seems your face is known to me.

MRS. LOVETT (*Concealing agitation*): Him? That's a laugh — him being my uncle's cousin and arrived from Birmingham yesterday.

TODD (*Very smooth*): But already, sir, I have heard Beadle Bamford spoken of with great respect.

BEADLE (*Whatever dim suspicions he may have had allayed by the flattery*): Well, sir, I try my best for my neighbors.

(*To* MRS. LOVETT)

Fleet Street? Over your pieshop, ma'am?

MRS. LOVETT: That's it, sir.

BEADLE: Then, Mr. Todd, you will surely see me there before the week is out.

TODD (*Expressionless*): You will be welcome, Beadle Bamford, and I guarantee to give you, without a penny's charge, the closest shave you will ever know.

(MRS. LOVETT *takes* TODD'*s arm and starts with him offstage as the scene blacks out. The factory whistle. In limbo, the* BEGGAR WOMAN *appears with other members of the company. They sing*)

MEMBERS OF THE COMPANY:

Sweeney pondered and Sweeney planned.

67

Like a perfect machine 'e planned,
Barbing the hook, baiting the trap,
Setting it out for the Beadle to snap.

Slyly courted 'im, Sweeney did,
Set a sort of a scene, 'e did.
Laying the trail, showing the traces,
Letting it lead to higher places . . .
Sweeney . . .

(*The lights shift to a room in* JUDGE TURPIN*'s house. The*
JUDGE *is in his judicial clothes, a Bible in his hand. In the*
adjoining room, JOHANNA *sits sewing*)

JUDGE (*Sings*):
Mea culpa, mea culpa,
Mea maxima culpa,
Mea maxima maxima culpa!
God deliver me! Release me!
Forgive me! Restrain me! Pervade me!
(*He peers through the keyhole of the door to* JOHANNA*'s*
room)
Johanna, Johanna,
So suddenly a woman,
The light behind your window —
It penetrates your gown . . .
Johanna, Johanna,
The sun — I see the sun through your —
(*Ashamed, he stops peering*)
No!
God!
Deliver me!
(*Sinks to his knees*)
Deliver me!
(*Starts tearing off his robes*)
Down!

68

Down.
Down . . .
   (*Now naked to the waist, he picks up a scourge from the table*)
Johanna, Johanna,
I watch you from the shadows.
You sigh before your window
And gaze upon the town . . .
Your lips part, Johanna,
So young and soft and beautiful —
                        (*Whips himself*)
God!
                  (*Again and again, as he continues*)
Deliver me!
Filth
Leave me!
Johanna!
Johanna!
I treasured you in innocence
And loved you like a daughter.
You mock me, Johanna,
You tempt me with your innocence,
You tempt me with those quivering —
                        (*Whips himself*)
No!
                  (*Again and again*)
God!
Deliver me!
It will —
Stop —
Now! It will —
Stop —
Right —
Now.
Right —

69

Now.
Right —
Now . . .
   (*Calm again, having kneed his way over to the door, he peers through the keyhole*)
Johanna, Johanna,
I cannot keep you longer.
The world is at your window,
You want to fly away.
You stir me, Johanna,
So suddenly a woman,
I cannot watch you one more day — !
            (*Again whips himself into a frenzy*)
God!
Deliver me!
God!
Deliver me!
God!
Deliver —
                  (*Climaxes*)
God!!
   (*Panting, he relaxes; when he is in control again, he starts to dress*)
Johanna, Johanna,
I'll keep you here forever,
I'll wed you on the morrow.
Johanna, Johanna,
The world will never touch you,
I'll wed you on the morrow!
As years pass, Johanna,
You'll tend me in my solitude,
No longer as a daughter,
As a woman.
               (*He is fully dressed again*)
Johanna, Johanna,

I'll hold you here forever then,
You'll keep away from windows and
You'll
Deliver me,
Johanna,
From this
Hot
Red
Devil
With your
Soft
White
Cool
Virgin
Palms . . .

> (*Magisterial again, picking up the Bible, he produces a key and opens the door, the key forgotten, still in the lock.* JOHANNA *jumps up*)

JOHANNA: Father!

JUDGE: Johanna, I trust you've not been near the window again.

JOHANNA (*During this speech her eyes fall on the key in the lock*): Hardly, dear father, when it has been shuttered and barred these last three days.

JUDGE: How right I was to insist on such a precaution, for once again he has come, that conscienceless young sailor. Ten times has he been driven from my door and yet . . .
> (*Breaks off, gazing at her, smitten with lust*)
How sweet you look in that light muslin gown.

JOHANNA: 'Tis nothing but an old dress, father.

JUDGE: But fairer on your young form than wings on an angel . . . oh, if I were to think . . .

JOHANNA (*Demurely, moving to the door*): Think what, dear father?

JUDGE: If I were to think you encouraged this young rogue . . .

JOHANNA (*During this speech, she slips the key from the lock, hides it in her dress*): I? A maid trained from the cradle to find in modesty and obedience the greatest of all virtues? Dear father, when have you ceased to warn me of the wickedness of men?

JUDGE: Venal young men of the street with only one thought in their heads. But there are men of different and far higher breed. I have one in mind for you.

JOHANNA: You have?

JUDGE: A gentle man, who would shield you from all earthly cares and guide your faltering steps to the sober warmth of womanhood — a husband — a protector — and yet an ardent lover too. It is a man who through all the years has surely earned your affection.
(*Drops to his knees*)

JOHANNA (*Staggered*): You?!!!
(*The scene blacks out*)

(*Light comes up on* MRS. LOVETT*'s pieshop and the apartment above, which now is sparsely furnished with a washstand and a long wooden chest. At the foot of the outside staircase is a brand-new barber's pole. Attached to the first banister of the staircase is an iron bell.* TODD *is pacing in the apartment above.* MRS. LOVETT *comes hurrying out of the shop, carrying a wooden chair. As she does so, the* BEGGAR WOMAN *shuffles up to her*)

BEGGAR WOMAN (*Sings*):
Alms . . . alms . . .

MRS. LOVETT (*Imitating her nastily, sings*):
Alms . . . alms . . .

72

(Music continues)

How many times have I told you? I'll not have trash from the gutter hanging around my establishment!

BEGGAR WOMAN: Not just a penny, dear? Or a pie? One of them pies that give the stomach cramps to half the neighborhood?
(A cackling laugh)
Come on, dear. Have a heart, dear.

MRS. LOVETT: Off. Off with you or you'll get a kick on the rump that'll make your teeth chatter!

BEGGAR WOMAN: Stuck up thing! You and your fancy airs!
(Shuffling off into the wings, sings)
Alms . . . alms . . .
For a desperate woman . . .
(Exits. Music continues. MRS. LOVETT rings the bell to indicate her approach and starts climbing the stairs. At the sound of the bell, TODD alerts and snatches up a razor. The music becomes agitated. As MRS. LOVETT appears, he relaxes somewhat. MRS. LOVETT is now very proprietary towards him)

MRS. LOVETT: It's not much of a chair, but it'll do till you get your fancy new one. It was me poor Albert's chair, it was. Sat in it all day long he did, after his leg give out from the dropsy.
(Surveying the room, music under)
Kinda bare, isn't it? I never did like a bare room. Oh, well, we'll find some nice little knickknacks.

TODD: Why doesn't the Beadle come? "Before the week is out," that's what he said.

MRS. LOVETT: And who says the week's out yet? It's only Tuesday.
(As TODD paces restlessly, sings)
Easy now.

73

Hush, love, hush.
Don't distress yourself,
What's your rush?
Keep your thoughts
Nice and lush.
Wait.
> (TODD *continues to pace*)

Hush, love, hush.
Think it through.
Once it bubbles,
Then what's to do?
Watch it close.
Let it brew.
Wait.
> (*Looking round, cheerfully, as* TODD *grows calmer*)

I've been thinking, flowers —
Maybe daisies —
To brighten up the room.
Don't you think some flowers,
Pretty daisies,
Might relieve the gloom?
> (*As* TODD *doesn't respond*)

Ah, wait, love, wait.
> (*Music continues under*)

TODD (*Intensely*): And the Judge? When will I get him?

MRS. LOVETT: Can't you think of nothing else? Always brood-in' away on yer wrongs what happened heaven knows how many years ago —
> (TODD *turns away violently with a hiss*)

Slow, love, slow.
Time's so fast.
Now goes quickly —
See, now it's past!
Soon will come.
Soon will last.

Wait.

> (TODD *grows calm again*)

Don't you know,
Silly man,
Half the fun is to
Plan the plan?
All good things come to
Those who can
Wait.

> (*Looking around the room again*)

Gillyflowers, maybe,
'Stead of daisies . . .
I don't know, though . . .
What do you think?

TODD (*Docilely*): Yes.

MRS. LOVETT (*Gently taking the razor from him*): Gillyflowers,
I'd say. Nothing like a nice bowl of gillies.

> (*Music stops. During the above, we have seen* ANTHONY
> *moving down the street. He sees the sign and stops. He goes
> to the bell and rings it, then starts running up the stairs.
> The effect on* TODD *is electric. Even* MRS. LOVETT, *affected
> by his tension, alerts. She hastily gives him back the razor.*
> ANTHONY *bursts in enthusiastically*)

TODD: Anthony.

ANTHONY: Mr. Todd. I've paced Fleet Street a dozen times
with no success. But now the sign! In business already.

TODD: Yes.

ANTHONY: I congratulate you.

> (*Turning to* MRS. LOVETT)

And . . . er . . .

MRS. LOVETT: Mrs. Lovett, sir.

ANTHONY: A pleasure, ma'am. Oh, Mr. Todd, I have so much

to tell you. I have found the fairest and most loving maid that any man could dream of! And yet there are problems. She has a guardian so tyrannical that she is kept shut up from human eye. But now this morning this key fell from her shuttered window.

(*He holds up* JOHANNA *'s key*)

The surest sign that Johanna loves me and . . .

MRS. LOVETT: Johanna?

ANTHONY: That's her name, ma'am, and Turpin that of the abominable parent. A judge, it seems. But, as I said, a monstrous tyrant. Oh Mr. Todd, once the Judge has gone to court, I'll slip into the house and plead with her to fly with me tonight. Yet when I have her — where can I bring her till I have hired a coach to speed us home to Plymouth? Oh Mr. Todd, if I could lodge her here just for an hour or two!

(*He gazes at the inscrutable* TODD)

MRS. LOVETT (*After a beat*): Bring her, dear.

ANTHONY: Oh thank you, thank you, ma'am.

(*To* TODD)

I have your consent, Mr. Todd?

TODD (*After a pause*): The girl may come.

(ANTHONY *grabs his hand and pumps it, then turns to grab* MRS. LOVETT *'s*)

ANTHONY: I shall be grateful for this to the grave. Now I must hurry, for surely the Judge is off to the Old Bailey.

(*Turning at the door*)

My thanks! A thousand blessings on you both!

(*He hurries out and down the stairs*)

MRS. LOVETT: Johanna! Who'd have thought it! It's like Fate, isn't it? You'll have her back before the day is out.

76

TODD: For a few hours? Before he carries her off to the other end of England?

MRS. LOVETT: Oh, that sailor! Let him bring her here and then, since you're so hot for a little . . .
(*Makes a throat-cutting gesture*)
. . . that's the throat to slit, dear. Oh Mr. T., we'll make a lovely home for her. You and me. The poor thing! All those years and not a scrap of motherly affection! I'll soon change that, I will, for if ever there was a maternal heart, it's mine.
(*During this speech* PIRELLI, *accompanied by* TOBIAS, *has appeared on the street. They see the sign and start up the stairs without ringing the bell. Now, as* MRS. LOVETT *goes to* TODD *coquettishly,* PIRELLI *and* TOBIAS *suddenly appear at the door.* TODD *pulls violently away from* MRS. LOVETT)

PIRELLI (*With Italianate bow*): Good morning, Mr. Todd — and to you, bellissima signorina.
(*He kisses* MRS. LOVETT*'s hand*)

MRS. LOVETT: Well, 'ow do you do, signor, I'm sure.

PIRELLI: A little business with Mr. Todd, signora. Perhaps if you will give the permission?

MRS. LOVETT: Oh yes, indeed, I'll just pop on down to my pies.
(*Surveying* TOBIAS)
Oh lawks, look at it now! Don't look like it's had a kind word since half past never!
(*Smiling at him*)
What would you say, son, to a nice juicy meat pie, eh? Your teeth is strong, I hope?

TOBIAS: Oh yes, ma'am.

MRS. LOVETT (*Taking his hand*): Then come with me, love.
(*They start down the stairs to the shop*)

77

PIRELLI: Mr. Todd.

TODD: Signor Pirelli.

PIRELLI (*Reverting to Irish*): Ow, call me Danny, Daniel O'Higgins' the name when it's not perfessional.
(*Looks around the shop*)
Not much, but I imagine you'll pretty it up a bit.
(*Holds out his hand*)
I'd like me five quid back, if'n ya don't mind.

TODD: Why?
(*In the shop,* MRS. LOVETT *pats a stool for* TOBIAS *to sit down and hands him a piece of pie. He starts to eat greedily*)

MRS. LOVETT: That's my boy. Tuck in.

PIRELLI: It'll hold me over till your customers start coming. Then it's half your profits you'll hand over to me every week on a Friday, share and share alike. All right . . . Mr. Benjamin Barker?

TODD (*Very quiet*): Why do you call me that?

MRS. LOVETT (*Stroking* TOBIAS'*s luxurious locks*): At least you've got a nice full head of hair on you.

TODD: Well, ma'am, to tell the truth, ma'am —
(*He reaches up and pulls off the "locks" which are a wig, revealing his own short-cropped hair*)
— gets awful 'ot.
(*He continues to eat the pie.* PIRELLI *strolls over to the washstand, picks up the razor, flicks it open*)

PIRELLI: You don't remember me. Why should you? I was just a down and out Irish lad you hired for a couple of weeks — sweeping up hair and such like —
(*Holding up razor*)
but I remember these — and you. Benjamin Barker, later transported to Botany Bay for life. So, Mr. Todd — is it a

deal or do I run down the street for me pal Beadle
Bamford?

(*For a long moment* TODD *stands gazing at him*)

PIRELLI (*Sings, nastily*):
You t'ink-a you smart,
You foolish-a boy.
Tomorrow you start
In my-a employ!
You unner-a-stan'?
You like-a my plan — ?
   (*Once again he hits his high note, and once again he is
   interrupted —* TODD *knocks the razor out of his hand and
   starts, in a protracted struggle, to strangle him*)

TOBIAS (*Downstairs, unaware of this*): Oh gawd, he's got an
appointment with his tailor. If he's late and it's my fault
— you don't know him!
   (*He jumps up and starts out*)

MRS. LOVETT: I wouldn't want to, I'm sure, dear.
   (TODD *violently continues with the strangling*)

TOBIAS (*Calling on the stairs*): Signor! It's late! The tailor, sir.
   (*Remembering*)
Oh, me wig!
   (*Runs back for it. Upstairs,* TODD *stops dead at the sound
   of the voice. He looks around wildly, sees the chest, runs to
   it, opens the lid and then drags* PIRELLI *to it and tumbles
   him in, slamming the lid shut just as* TOBIAS *enters. It is
   at this moment that we realize that one of* PIRELLI*'s hands
   is dangling out of the chest*)
Signor, I did like you said. I reminded you . . . the tailor
. . . Ow, he ain't here.

TODD: Signor Pirelli has been called away.

TOBIAS: Where did he go?

TODD: He didn't say. You'd better run after him.

79

TOBIAS: Oh no, sir. Knowing him, sir, without orders to the contrary, I'd best wait for him *here*.

(*He crosses to the chest and sits down on it, perilously near* PIRELLI's *hand, which he doesn't notice.* TODD *at this moment does, however. Suddenly he is all nervous smiles*)

TODD: So Mrs. Lovett gave you a pie, did she, my lad?

TOBIAS: Oh yes, sir. She's a real kind lady. One whole pie.

(*As he speaks, his hand moves very close to* PIRELLI's *hand*)

TODD (*Moving toward him*): A whole pie, eh? That's a treat. And yet, if I know a growing boy, there's still room for more, eh?

TOBIAS: I'd say, sir.

(*Patting his stomach*)

An aching void.

(*Once again his hand is on the edge of the chest, moving toward* PIRELLI's *hand. Slowly now, we see the fingers of* PIRELLI's *hand stirring, feebly trying to clutch* TOBIAS's *hand. When it has almost reached him,* TODD *grabs* TOBIAS *up off the chest*)

TODD: Then why don't you run downstairs and wait for your master there? There'll be another pie in it for you, I'm sure.

(*Afterthought*)

And tell Mrs. Lovett to give you a nice big tot of gin.

TOBIAS: Oo, sir! Gin, sir! Thanking you, sir, thanking you kindly. Gin! You're a Christian indeed, sir!

(*He runs down the stairs to* MRS. LOVETT)

Oh, ma'am, the gentleman says to give me a nice tot of gin, ma'am.

MRS. LOVETT: Gin, dear? Why not?

(*Upstairs, with great ferocity,* TODD *opens the chest, grabs the screaming* PIRELLI *by the hair, tugs him up from the*

chest and slashes his throat as, downstairs, MRS. LOVETT
pours a glass of gin and hands it to TOBIAS. *He takes it.*
The tableau freezes, then fades)

THREE TENORS (*Enter and sing*):
His hands were quick, his fingers strong.
It stung a little but not for long.
And those who thought him a simple clod
Were soon reconsidering under the sod,
Consigned there with a friendly prod
From Sweeney Todd,
The Demon Barber of Fleet Street.

See your razor gleam, Sweeney,
Feel how well it fits
As it floats across the throats
Of hypocrites . . .

(*The ballad ends on a crashing chord as the singers black
out and light comes up on* JUDGE TURPIN *in full panoply
of wig, robe, etc. He is about to convict a young boy*)

JUDGE: This is the fourth time, sir, that you have been
brought before this bench. Though it is my earnest wish
ever to temper justice with mercy, your persistent dedica-
tion to a life of crime is such an abomination before God
and man that I have no alternative but to sentence you to
hang by the neck until you are dead.
(*He produces the black cap and puts it on his head. As he
does so the condemned prisoner is led away*)
Court adjourned.
(*During the following, the* JUDGE *removes cap, wig, and
gown. To the* BEADLE)
It is perhaps remiss of me to close the court so early, but
the stench of those miserable wretches at the bar was so
offensive to my nostrils I feared my eagerness for fresher
air might well impair the soundness of my judgement.

81

(*Light dims on the court and finds the* JUDGE *and the* BEA-DLE *now walking down a street together*)

BEADLE: Well, sir, the adjournment is fortunate for me, sir, for it's today we celebrate my sweet little Annie's birthday, and to have her daddy back so soon to hug and kiss her will be her crowning joy on such a happy day.

JUDGE: It is a happy moment for me, too. Walk home with me for I have news for you. In order to shield her from the evils of this world, I have decided to marry Johanna next Monday.

BEADLE: Ah, sir, happy news indeed.

JUDGE: Strange, when I offered myself to her, she showed a certain reluctance. But that's natural enough in a young girl. Now that she has had time for reflection, I'm sure she will greet my proposal in a more sensible frame of mind.

(*Light leaves them and comes up on* JOHANNA *and* ANTHONY *in* JOHANNA*'s room. She is pacing in agitation and fear*)

JOHANNA (*Sings*):
He means to marry me Monday,
What shall I do? I'd rather die.

ANTHONY (*Sings*):
I have a plan —

JOHANNA:
I'll swallow poison on Sunday,
That's what I'll do, I'll get some lye.

ANTHONY:
I have a plan —

JOHANNA (*Stops pacing suddenly*):
Oh, dear, was that a noise?

82

ANTHONY:
A plan —

JOHANNA:
I think I heard a noise.

ANTHONY:
A plan!

JOHANNA:
It couldn't be,
He's in court,
He's in court today,
Still that was a noise,
Wasn't that a noise?
You must have heard that —

ANTHONY:
Kiss me.

JOHANNA (*Shyly*):
Oh, sir . . .

ANTHONY:
Ah, miss . . .

JOHANNA:
Oh, sir . . .
                    (*She turns away, agitatedly*)
If he should marry me Monday,
What shall I do? I'll die of grief.

ANTHONY:
We fly tonight —

JOHANNA:
'Tis Friday, virtually Sunday,
What can we do with time so brief?

ANTHONY:
We fly tonight —

JOHANNA:
  Behind the curtain — quick!

ANTHONY:
  Tonight —

JOHANNA:
  I think I heard a click!

ANTHONY:
  Tonight!

JOHANNA:
It was a gate!
It's the gate!   ANTHONY:
We don't have a gate.   It's not a gate.
Still there was a — Wait!   There's no gate,
There's another click!   You don't have a gate.
You must have heard that — If you'd only listen, miss, and —

ANTHONY:
  Kiss me!

JOHANNA:
  Tonight?

ANTHONY:
  Kiss me.

JOHANNA:
  You mean tonight?

ANTHONY:
  The plan is made.

JOHANNA:
  Oh, sir!

ANTHONY:
  So kiss me.

JOHANNA:
  I feel a fright.

84

ANTHONY:
Be not afraid.

JOHANNA:	ANTHONY:
Sir, I did	Tonight I'll
Love you even as I	Steal
Saw you, even as it	You,
Did not matter that I	Johanna,
Did not know your name.	I'll steal you . . .

ANTHONY:
It's me you'll marry on Monday,
That's what you'll do!

JOHANNA:
And gladly, sir.

ANTHONY:
St. Dunstan's, noon.

JOHANNA:	
I knew I'd be with you one day,	
Even not knowing who you were.	ANTHONY:
I feared you'd never come,	Ah, miss,
That you'd been called away,	Marry me, marry me, miss,
That you'd been killed,	Oh, marry me Monday!
Had the plague,	Favor me, favor me
Were in debtor's jail,	With your hand.
Trampled by a horse,	Promise,
Gone to sea again,	Marry me, marry me, please,
Arrested by the —	Oh, marry me Monday —

JOHANNA:
Kiss me!

ANTHONY:
Of course.

JOHANNA:
Quickly!

85

ANTHONY:
　　You're sure?

JOHANNA:
　　Kiss me!

ANTHONY (*Taking her in his arms*):
　　I shall!

JOHANNA:
　　Kiss me!
　　Oh, sir . . .

　　　(*Lights dim on them but remain; light rises on the* JUDGE
　　　and the BEADLE, *still walking together. Music continues
　　　under*)

JUDGE (*Strolling with* BEADLE): Yes, yes, but surely the respect
　　that she owes me as her guardian should be sufficient to
　　kindle a more tender emotion.

BEADLE (*Sings*):
　　Excuse me, my lord.
　　May I request, my lord,
　　Permission, my lord, to speak?
　　Forgive me if I suggest, my lord,
　　You're looking less than your best, my lord,
　　There's powder upon your vest, my lord,
　　And stubble upon your cheek.
　　And ladies, my lord, are weak.
　　　　　　　(*Music continues*)

JUDGE: Perhaps if she greets me cordially upon my return, I
　　should give her a small gift . . .

BEADLE (*Winces delicately*):
　　Ladies in their sensitivities, my lord,
　　Have a fragile sensibility.
　　When a girl's emergent,

86

Probably it's urgent
You defer to her gent-
Ility, my lord.
Personal disorder cannot be ignored,
Given their genteel proclivities.
Meaning no offense, it
Happens they resents it,
Ladies in their sensit-
Ivities, my lord.

JUDGE (*Feeling his chin*): Stubble, you say? Perhaps at times I am a little overhasty with my morning ablutions . . .

BEADLE:
Fret not though, my lord,
I know a place, my lord,
A barber, my lord, of skill.
Thus armed with a shaven face, my lord,
Some eau de cologne to grace my lord
And musk to enhance the chase, my lord,
You'll dazzle the girl until
She bows to your every will.

JUDGE: That may well be so.
> (*They have reached the* JUDGE*'s house*)

BEADLE: Well, here we are, sir. I bid you good day.

JUDGE: Good day.
> (*He muses, turns*)
And where is this miraculous barber?

BEADLE: In Fleet Street, sir.

JUDGE: Perhaps you may be right. Take me to him.
> (*They start off. Light up on* JOHANNA*'s room.* JOHANNA *and* ANTHONY *get up from a couch*)

BEADLE (*Sings*):
The name is Todd . . .

JUDGE:
    Todd, eh?

ANTHONY:
    We'd best not wait until Monday

            JOHANNA:
Sir, I concur,   BEADLE:
And fully, too.   Sweeney Todd.

ANTHONY:
    It isn't right.
    We'd best be married on Sunday.

JOHANNA:
    Saturday, sir,
    Would also do.

ANTHONY:
    Or else tonight.
            (*The* JUDGE *and the* BEADLE *move past the house*)

JOHANNA:
    I think I heard a noise.

ANTHONY:
    Fear not.

JOHANNA:
    I mean another noise!

ANTHONY:
    Like what?

            JOHANNA:
Oh, never mind,
Just a noise
Just another noise,   ANTHONY:
Something in the street,   You mustn't mind,
I'm a silly little   It's a noise,
Ninnynoddle —   Just another noise,
                             Something in the street,
                             You silly —

BOTH (*Falling into each other's arms*):
  Kiss me!

JOHANNA:
  Oh, sir . . .

ANTHONY:
  We'll go to Paris on Monday.

JOHANNA:
  What shall I wear?
  I daren't pack!

ANTHONY:
  We'll ride a train . . .

JOHANNA:
  With you beside me on Sunday,
  What will I care
  What things I lack?

ANTHONY:
  Then sail to Spain . . .

JOHANNA:	ANTHONY:
I'll take my reticule.	
I need my reticule.	Why take your reticule?
You mustn't think	We'll buy a reticule.
Me a fool	I'd never think
But my reticule	You a fool,
Never leaves my side,	But a reticule —
It's the only thing	Leave it all aside
My mother gave me —	And begin again and
Kiss me!	Kiss me!
Kiss me!	
	I know a place where we can go
We'll go there,	Tonight.
Kiss me!	Kiss me!
We have a place where we can	We have a place where we can

89

Go . . .   Go tonight.

BEADLE (*Simultaneously with the above*):
  The name is Todd.

JUDGE:
  Todd?

BEADLE:
  Todd. Sweeney Todd.

JUDGE:
  Todd . . .

BEADLE:
  Todd.

JOHANNA:	ANTHONY:
I loved you	I loved you
Even as I saw you,	Even as I saw you,
Even as it does not	Even as it did not
Matter that I still	Matter that I did
Don't know your name, sir,	Not know your name . . .
Even as I saw you,	
Even as it does not	Johanna . . .
Matter that I still	Johanna . . .
Don't know your name . . .	Johanna . . .

BEADLE (*Simultaneously with above*):
  Todd . . . Sweeney Todd.

JUDGE *and* BEADLE:
  Sweeney Todd.

ANTHONY: Anthony . . .

JUDGE: Todd . . .

BEADLE: Todd.

JOHANNA: Anthony . . .

JUDGE: Todd, eh?

JOHANNA:	ANTHONY:
I'll marry Anthony Sunday,	You marry Anthony Sunday,
That's what I'll do,	That's what you'll do,
No matter what!	No matter what!
I knew you'd come for me one day,	I knew I'd come for you one day
Only afraid that you'd forgot.	Only afraid that you'd forgot.

BEADLE (*Simultaneously with above*):
  Ladies in their sensitivities, my lord . . .

JUDGE:
  Pray lead the way.

BEADLE:
  Have a fragile sensibility . . .

JUDGE:
  Just as you say.

JOHANNA:	ANTHONY:
I feared you'd never come,	Marry me, marry me, miss,
That you'd been called away,	You'll marry me Sunday.
That you'd been killed,	Favor me, favor me
Had the plague,	With your hand.
Were in debtor's jail,	Promise,
Trampled by a horse,	Marry me, marry me,
Gone to sea again,	That you'll marry me —
Arrested by the . . .	Enough of all this . . .

(*He crushes her to him; they kiss*)

BEADLE (*Simultaneously with above*):
  When a girl's emergent,
  Probably it's urgent . . .
  Ladies in their sensitivities . . .

JUDGE:
  Todd . . .

JOHANNA (*As she sinks to the floor with* ANTHONY):
Oh, sir . . .

ANTHONY:
Ah, miss . . .

JOHANNA:
Oh, sir . . .   ANTHONY:
Oh, sir . . .   Ah, miss . . .
Oh, sir . . .   Ah, miss . . .
Oh, sir . . .   Ah, miss . . .
Oh, sir . . .   Ah, miss . . .
Oh, sir . . .   Ah, miss . . .

> (*Light leaves them, comes up on the pieshop-tonsorial par-
> lor. Upstairs,* TODD *is silently cleaning his razor. In the
> shop,* MRS. LOVETT *and* TOBIAS *unfreeze from the position
> in which they were last seen*)

MRS. LOVETT: Maybe you should run along, dear.

TOBIAS: Oh no, ma'am, I daren't budge till he calls for me.

MRS. LOVETT: I'll pop up and see what Mr. Todd says.
> (*Humming,* MRS. LOVETT *starts climbing the stairs. As she
> enters the parlor*)
Ah me, my poor knees is not what they was, dear.
> (*She sits down on the chest*)
How long before the Eyetalian gets back?

TODD (*Still impassively cleaning the razor*): He won't be back.

MRS. LOVETT (*Instantly suspicious*): Now, Mr. T., you didn't!
> (TODD *nods toward the chest. Realizing,* MRS. LOVETT *jumps
> up. For a moment she stands looking at the chest, then, gin-
> gerly, she lifts the lid. She gazes down, then spins to* TODD)
You're crazy mad! Killing a man wot done you no harm?
And the boy downstairs?

TODD: He recognized me from the old days. He tried to

blackmail me, half my earnings forever.

MRS. LOVETT: Oh well, that's a different matter! What a relief, dear! For a moment I thought you'd lost your marbles.
>   (*Turns to peer down again into the chest*)
Ooh! All that blood! Enough to make you come all over gooseflesh, ain't it. Poor bugger. Oh, well!
>   (*She starts to close the lid, sees something, bends to pick it up. It is* PIRELLI*'s purse. She looks in it*)
Three quid! Well, waste not, want not, as I always say.
>   (*She takes out the money and puts it down her bosom. She is about to throw the purse away when something about it attracts her. She slips it too down her dress. She shuts the chest lid and, quite composed again, sits down on it*)
Now, dear, we got to use the old noggin.
>   (*As she sits deep in thought, we see the* JUDGE *and* BEADLE *coming up the street*)

BEADLE (*Pointing*): There you are, sir. Above the pieshop, sir.

JUDGE: I see. You may leave me now.

BEADLE: Thank you, sir. Thank you.
>   (*He starts off as the* JUDGE *approaches the parlor*)

MRS. LOVETT (*Coming out of her pondering*): Well, first there's the lad.

TODD: Send him up here.

MRS. LOVETT: Him, too! Now surely one's enough for today, dear. Shouldn't indulge yourself, you know. Now let me see, he's half seas over already with the gin . . .
>   (*As she speaks, downstairs the* JUDGE *clangs the bell.* TODD *runs to the landing and peers down the stairs. The* BEADLE *is still visible, exiting*)

TODD: Providence is kind!

MRS. LOVETT: Who is it?

TODD: Judge Turpin.

MRS. LOVETT (*Flustered*): Him, him? The Judge? It can't be! It —

TODD: Quick, leave me!

MRS. LOVETT: What are you going to do?

TODD (*Roaring*): Leave me, I said!

MRS. LOVETT: Don't worry, dear. I'm — out!
(*She scuttles out of the tonsorial parlor and starts down the stairs as the* JUDGE *ascends. They meet halfway. She gives him a deep curtsy*)
Excuse me, your Lordship.
(*She hurries back to* TOBIAS *in the shop*)

JUDGE: Mr. Todd?

TODD: At your service, sir. An honor to receive your patronage, sir.

MRS. LOVETT (*To* TOBIAS): Now, dear, seems like your guvnor has gone and left you high and dry. But don't worry. Your Aunt Nellie will think of what to do with you.
(*Picks up the bottle of gin and pours some more into his glass. Still holding the bottle, she leads him toward the curtains*)
Come on into my lovely back parlor.
(*They disappear through the curtain*)

JUDGE (*Looking around*): These premises are hardly prepossessing and yet the Beadle tells me you are the most accomplished of all the barbers in the city.

TODD: That is gracious of him, sir. And you must please excuse the modesty of my establishment. It's only a few days ago that I set up quarters here and some necessaries are yet to come.
(*Indicating chair*)

94

Sit, sir, if you please, sir. Sit.
> (*The* JUDGE *settles into the chair; music under as* MRS. LOVETT, *still holding the gin bottle, enters her back parlor with* TOBIAS)

MRS. LOVETT: See how nice and cozy it is? Sit down, dear, sit.
> (*She starts to pour him more gin*)

Oh, it's empty. Now you just sit there, dear, like a good quiet boy while I get a new bottle from the larder.
> (*She leaves him alone*)

TODD: And what may I do for you, sir? A stylish trimming of the hair? A soothing skin massage?

JUDGE (*Sings*):
> You see, sir, a man infatuate with love,
> Her ardent and eager slave.
> So fetch the pomade and pumice stone
> And lend me a more seductive tone,
> A sprinkling perhaps of French cologne,
> But first, sir, I think — a shave.

TODD: The closest I ever gave.
> (*He whips the sheet over the* JUDGE, *then tucks the bib in. The* JUDGE *hums, flicking imaginary dust off the sheet;* TODD *whistles gaily*)

JUDGE: You are in a merry mood today, Mr. Todd.

TODD (*Sings, mixing lather*):
> 'Tis your delight, sir, catching fire
> From one man to the next.

JUDGE:
> 'Tis true, sir, love can still inspire
> The blood to pound, the heart leap higher.

BOTH:
> What more, what more can man require —

JUDGE:

Than love, sir?

TODD:

More than love, sir.

JUDGE:

What, sir?

TODD:

Women.

JUDGE:

Ah yes, women.

TODD:

Pretty women.

(*The* JUDGE *hums jauntily;* TODD *whistles and starts stropping his razor rhythmically. He then lathers the* JUDGE's *face. Still whistling, he stands back to survey the* JUDGE, *who is now totally relaxed, eyes closed. He picks up the razor and sings to it*)

Now then, my friend.

Now to your purpose.

Patience, enjoy it.

Revenge can't be taken in haste.

JUDGE (*Opens his eyes*):

Make haste, and if we wed,

You'll be commended, sir.

TODD (*Bows*):

My lord . . .

(*Goes to him*)

And who, may it be said,

Is your intended, sir?

JUDGE:

My ward.

96

(TODD *freezes; the* JUDGE *closes his eyes, settles comfortably, speaks*)

And pretty as a rosebud.

TODD (*Music rising*): As pretty as her mother?

JUDGE (*Mildly puzzled*): What? What was that?
  (*As the music reaches a shrill crescendo,* TODD *is slowly bringing the razor toward the* JUDGE*'s throat when suddenly the* JUDGE *opens his eyes and starts to twist around in curiosity*)

TODD (*Musingly, lightly*): Oh, nothing, sir. Nothing. May we proceed?
  (*Starts to shave the* JUDGE, *sings*)

Pretty women . . .
Fascinating . . .
Sipping coffee,
Dancing . . .
Pretty women
Are a wonder.
Pretty women.

Sitting in the window or
Standing on the stair,
Something in them
Cheers the air.

Pretty women . . .

JUDGE:
Silhouetted . . .

TODD:
Stay within you . . .

JUDGE:
Glancing . . .

TODD:
Stay forever . . .

JUDGE:
Breathing lightly . . .

TODD:
Pretty women . . .

BOTH:
Pretty women!
Blowing out their candles or
Combing out their hair . . .

JUDGE:
Then they leave . . .
Even when they leave you
And vanish, they somehow
Can still remain
There with you,
There with you.

TODD:
Even when they leave,
They still
Are
There.
They're there.

BOTH:
Ah,
Pretty women . . .

TODD:
At their mirrors . . .

JUDGE:
In their gardens . . .

TODD:
Letter-writing . . .

JUDGE:
Flower-picking . . .

TODD:
Weather-watching . . .

BOTH:
How they make a man sing!

Proof of heaven
As you're living —
Pretty women, sir!

JUDGE:	TODD:
Pretty women, yes!	Pretty women, here's to
Pretty women, sir!	Pretty women, all the
Pretty women!	Pretty women . . .
Pretty women, sir!	

    (TODD *raises his arm in a huge arc and is about to slice the razor across the* JUDGE*'s throat when* ANTHONY *bursts in*)

ANTHONY (*Singing*):
She says she'll marry me Sunday,
Everything's set, we leave tonight — !

JUDGE (*Jumping up, spilling the basin and knocking the razor from* TODD*'s hand*): You!

ANTHONY: Judge Turpin!

JUDGE: There is indeed a Higher Power to warn me thus in time.
    (*As* ANTHONY *retreats, he jumps on him and grabs him by the arm*)
Johanna elope with you? Deceiving slut — I'll lock her up in some obscure retreat where neither you nor any other vile, corrupting youth shall ever lay eyes on her again.

ANTHONY (*Shaking himself free*): But, sir, I beg of you —

JUDGE (*To* TODD): And as for you, barber, it is all too clear what company you keep. Service them well and hold their custom — for you'll have none of mine.
    (*He strides out and down the stairs*)

ANTHONY: Mr. Todd!

TODD (*Shouting*): Out! Out, I say!

(*Bewildered,* ANTHONY *leaves. Music begins under, very agitated.* TODD *stands motionless, in shock. As the* JUDGE *hurries off down the street,* MRS. LOVETT, *with a new bottle of gin in her hand, sees him. She glances after him, then goes into the back parlor where* TOBIAS *is now asleep. She looks at him, puts down the bottle and hurries out and up the stairs to* TODD)

MRS. LOVETT: All this running and shouting. What is it now, dear?

TODD: I had him — and then . . .

MRS. LOVETT: The sailor busted in. I saw them both running down the street and I said to myself: "The fat's in the fire, for sure!"

TODD (*Interrupting, sings*):
I had him!
His throat was bare
Beneath my hand — !

MRS. LOVETT (*Alarmed, pacifying*): There, there, dear. Don't fret.

TODD:
No, I had him!
His throat was there,
And he'll never come again!

MRS. LOVETT:
Easy now.
Hush, love, hush.
I keep telling you —

TODD (*Violently*):
When?

MRS. LOVETT:
What's your rush?

TODD:

    Why did I wait?

    You told me to wait!

    Now he'll never come again!

        (*Music becomes ferocious.* TODD*'s insanity, always close to
        the surface, explodes finally*)

    There's a hole in the world

    Like a great black pit

    And it's filled with people

    Who are filled with shit

    And the vermin of the world

    Inhabit it —

    But not for long!

    They all deserve to die!

    Tell you why, Mrs. Lovett,

    Tell you why:

    Because in all of the whole human race, Mrs. Lovett,

    There are two kinds of men and only two.

    There's the one staying put

    In his proper place

    And the one with his foot

    In the other one's face —

    Look at me, Mrs. Lovett,

    Look at you!

    No, we all deserve to die!

    Tell you why, Mrs. Lovett,

    Tell you why:

    Because the lives of the wicked should be —

                (*Slashes at the air*)

    Made brief.

    For the rest of us, death

    Will be a relief —

    We all deserve to die!

             (*Keening*)

And I'll never see Johanna,
No, I'll never hug my girl to me —
Finished!
                    (*Turns on the audience*)
All right! You, sir,
How about a shave?
                    (*Slashes twice*)
Come and visit
Your good friend Sweeney — !
You, sir, too, sir —
Welcome to the grave!
I will have vengeance,
I will have salvation!

Who, sir? You, sir?
No one's in the chair —
Come on, come on,
Sweeney's waiting!
I want you bleeders!
You, sir — anybody!
Gentlemen, now don't be shy!
Not one man, no,
Nor ten men,
Nor a hundred
Can assuage me —
I will have you!
                    (*To* MRS. LOVETT)
And I *will* get him back
Even as he gloats.
In the meantime I'll practice
On less honorable throats.
                    (*Keening again*)
And my Lucy lies in ashes
And I'll never see my girl again,
But the work waits,
I'm alive at last

(Exalted)

And I'm full of joy!

(*He drops down into the barber's chair in a sweat, panting*)

MRS. LOVETT (*Who has been watching him intently*): That's all very well, but all that matters now is him!

(*She points to the chest.* TODD *still sits motionless. She goes to him, peers at him*)

Listen! Do you hear me? Can you hear me? Get control of yourself.

(*She slaps his cheek. After a long pause,* TODD, *still in a half-dream, gets to his feet*)

What are we going to do about him? And there's the lad downstairs. We'd better go and have a look and be sure he's still there. When I left him he was sound asleep in the parlor.

(*She starts downstairs*)

Come on!

(TODD *follows. She disappears into the back parlor and re-emerges*)

No problem there. He's still sleeping. He's simple as a baby lamb. Later I can fob him off with some story easy. But him!

(*Indicating the tonsorial parlor above*)

What are we going to do with him?

TODD (*Disinterestedly*): Later on, when it's dark, we'll take him to some secret place and bury him.

MRS. LOVETT: Well, of course, we could do that. I don't suppose there's any relatives going to come poking around looking for him. But . . .

(*Pause. Chord*)

You know me. Sometimes ideas just pop into me head and I keep thinking . . .

(*Sings*)

Seems a downright shame . . .

TODD: Shame?

MRS. LOVETT:

Seems an awful waste . . .
Such a nice plump frame
Wot's-his-name
Has . . .
Had . . .
Has . . .
Nor it can't be traced.
Business needs a lift —
Debts to be erased —
Think of it as thrift,
As a gift . . .
If you get my drift . . .
                    (TODD *stares into space*)
No?
                         (*She sighs*)
Seems an awful waste.
I mean,
With the price of meat what it is,
When you get it,
If you get it —

TODD (*Becoming aware, chuckling*): Ah!

MRS. LOVETT:

Good, you got it.
                    (*Warming to it*)
Take, for instance,
Mrs. Mooney and her pie shop.
Business never better, using only
Pussycats and toast.
And a pussy's good for maybe six or
Seven at the most.
And I'm sure they can't compare
As far as taste —

104

TODD:
Mrs. Lovett,
What a charming notion,   MRS. LOVETT:
Eminently practical and yet
Appropriate, as always.   Well, it does seem a
Mrs. Lovett   Waste . . .
How I've lived without you   It's an idea . . .
All these years I'll never know! Think about it . . .
How delectable!   Lots of other gentlemen'll
Also undetectable.   Soon be coming for a shave
                                  Won't they?
                                  Think of
How choice!   All them
How rare!   Pies!

TODD:
   For what's the sound of the world out there?

MRS. LOVETT:
   What, Mr. Todd,
   What, Mr. Todd,
   What is that sound?

TODD:
   Those crunching noises pervading the air?

MRS. LOVETT:
   Yes, Mr. Todd,
   Yes, Mr. Todd,
   Yes, all around —

        TODD:
It's man devouring man, my dear,   MRS. LOVETT:
And who are we   Then who are we
To deny it in here?   To deny it in here?

TODD: These are desperate times, Mrs. Lovett, and desperate measures are called for.

105

(*She goes to the counter and comes back with an imaginary pie*)

MRS. LOVETT: Here we are, hot from the oven.
(*She holds it out to him*)

TODD:
What is that?

MRS. LOVETT:
It's priest.
Have a little priest.

TODD:
Is it really good?

MRS. LOVETT:
Sir, it's too good,
At least.
Then again, they don't commit sins of the flesh,
So it's pretty fresh.

TODD (*Looking at it*):
Awful lot of fat.

MRS. LOVETT:
Only where it sat.

TODD:
Haven't you got poet
Or something like that?

MRS. LOVETT:
No, you see the trouble with poet
Is, how do you know it's
Deceased?
Try the priest.

TODD (*Tasting it*): Heavenly.
(MRS. LOVETT *giggles*)

106

Not as hearty as bishop, perhaps, but not as bland as curate, either.

MRS. LOVETT: And good for business — always leaves you wanting more. Trouble is, we only get it in Sundays . . .
(TODD *chuckles.* MRS. LOVETT *presents another imaginary pie*)
Lawyer's rather nice.

TODD:
If it's for a price.

MRS. LOVETT:
Order something else, though, to follow,
Since no one should swallow
It twice.

TODD:
Anything that's lean.

MRS. LOVETT:
Well, then, if you're British and loyal,
You might enjoy Royal
Marine.
(TODD *makes a face*)
Anyway, it's clean.
Though, of course, it tastes of wherever it's been.

TODD (*Looking past her at an imaginary oven*):
Is that squire
On the fire?

MRS. LOVETT:
Mercy no, sir,
Look closer,
You'll notice it's grocer.

TODD:
Looks thicker.
More like vicar.

MRS. LOVETT:
No, it has to be grocer — it's green.

TODD:
The history of the world, my love —

MRS. LOVETT:
Save a lot of graves,
Do a lot of relatives favors . . .

TODD:
— is those below serving those up above.

MRS. LOVETT:
Everybody shaves,
So there should be plenty of flavors . . .

TODD:
How gratifying for once to know —

BOTH:
— that those above will serve those down below!

MRS. LOVETT: Now, let's see . . .
(*Surveying an imaginary tray of pies on the counter*)
We've got tinker . . .

TODD (*Looking at it*): Something pinker.

MRS. LOVETT: Tailor?

TODD (*Shaking his head*): Paler.

MRS. LOVETT: Butler?

TODD: Subtler.

MRS. LOVETT: Potter?

TODD (*Feeling it*): Hotter.

MRS. LOVETT: Locksmith?
(TODD *shrugs, defeated.* MRS. LOVETT *offers another imaginary pie*)

108

Lovely bit of clerk.

TODD:
Maybe for a lark . . .

MRS. LOVETT:
Then again, there's sweep
If you want it cheap
And you like it dark.
                    (*Another*)
Try the financier.
Peak of his career.

TODD:
That looks pretty rank.

MRS. LOVETT:
Well, he drank.
It's a bank
Cashier.
Last one really sold.
                    (*Feels it*)
Wasn't quite so old.

TODD:
Have you any Beadle?

MRS. LOVETT:
Next week, so I'm told.
Beadle isn't bad till you smell it
And notice how well it's
Been greased.
Stick to priest.
                    (*Offers another pie*)
Now this may be a bit stringy, but then, of course, it's fid-
dle player.

TODD: This isn't fiddle player. It's piccolo player.

MRS. LOVETT: How can you tell?

TODD: It's piping hot.

(*Giggles*)

MRS. LOVETT (*Snorts with glee*): Then blow on it first.
(TODD *guffaws*)

TODD:
The history of the world, my sweet —

MRS. LOVETT:
Oh, Mr. Todd,
Ooh, Mr. Todd,
What does it tell?

TODD:
— is who gets eaten and who gets to eat.

MRS. LOVETT:
And, Mr. Todd,
Too, Mr. Todd,
Who gets to sell.

TODD:
But fortunately, it's also clear —

TODD:	MRS. LOVETT:
That everybody	But everybody
Goes down well with beer.	Goes down well with beer.

MRS. LOVETT: Since marine doesn't appeal to you, how about
rear admiral?

TODD: Too salty. I prefer general.

MRS. LOVETT: With or without his privates? "With" is extra.
(TODD *chortles*)

TODD (*As* MRS. LOVETT *offers another pie*):
What is that?

MRS. LOVETT:
It's fop.

Finest in the shop.
Or we have some shepherd's pie peppered
With actual shepherd
On top.
And I've just begun.
Here's the politician — so oily
It's served with a doily —
                    (TODD *makes a face*)
Have one.

TODD:
Put it on a bun.
                    (*As she looks at him quizzically*)
Well, you never know if it's going to run.

MRS. LOVETT:
Try the friar.
Fried, it's drier.

TODD:
No, the clergy is really
Too coarse and too mealy.

MRS. LOVETT:
Then actor —
That's compacter.

TODD:
Yes, and always arrives overdone.
I'll come again when you
Have Judge on the menu . . .

MRS. LOVETT: Wait! True, we don't have Judge — yet — but
would you settle for the next best thing?

TODD: What's that?

MRS. LOVETT (*Handing him a butcher's cleaver*): Executioner.
    (TODD *roars, and then, picking up her wooden rolling pin,
    hands it to her*)

111

TODD:

Have charity toward the world, my pet —

MRS. LOVETT:

Yes, yes, I know, my love —

TODD:

We'll take the customers that we can get.

MRS. LOVETT:

High-born and low, my love.

TODD:

We'll not discriminate great from small.
No, we'll serve anyone —
Meaning anyone —

BOTH:

And to anyone
At all!

(*Music continues as the two of them brandish their "wea-
pons." The scene blacks out.*)

The Prologue's front drop depicting in a honey-
comb the class system of mid-19th Century England

"The Worst Pies in London"
Mrs. Lovett (Angela Lansbury) and Sweeney Todd
(Len Cariou)

"My Friends"
Sweeney (Len Cariou)

MARTHA SWOPE

Johanna (Sarah Rice) and Anthony (Victor Garber)

"Pirelli's Miracle Elixir"
Tobias (Ken Jennings) and crowd

117

"The Contest"
Mrs. Lovett (Angela Lansbury, *far left*), Sweeney (Len
Cariou), customer (Frank Kopyc, *seated*), Pirelli (Joaquin
Romaguera, *above center*), customer (Duane Bodin, *seated*)
Tobias (Ken Jennings) and crowd

MARTHA SWOPE

119

"Wait"
Mrs. Lovett (Angela Lansbury) and Sweeney (Len Cariou)

"Johanna"
Judge Turpin (Edmund Lyndeck) and Johanna (Sarah Rice)

MARTHA SWOPE

"Kiss Me" and *"Ladies in Their Sensitivities"*
Johanna (Sarah Rice) and Anthony (Victor Garber) and
(*top*) Judge Turpin (Edmund Lyndeck) and the Beadle
(Jack Eric Williams)

"Pretty Women"
Sweeney (Len Cariou) and Judge Turpin (Edmund Lyndeck)

"A Little Priest"
Mrs. Lovett (Angela Lansbury) and Sweene
(Len Cariou)

MARTHA SWOPE

"God, That's Good!"
Mrs. Lovett (Angela Lansbury), Sweeney
(Len Cariou, *above right*) and customers

"Johanna"
Johanna (Sarah Rice, *far left behind bars*), Anthony
(Victor Garber), and Sweeney (Len Cariou)

VAN WILLIAMS

"By the Sea"
Mrs. Lovett (Angela Lansbury)

130

"Not While I'm Around"
Tobias (Ken Jennings) and Mrs. Lovett (Angela Lansbury)

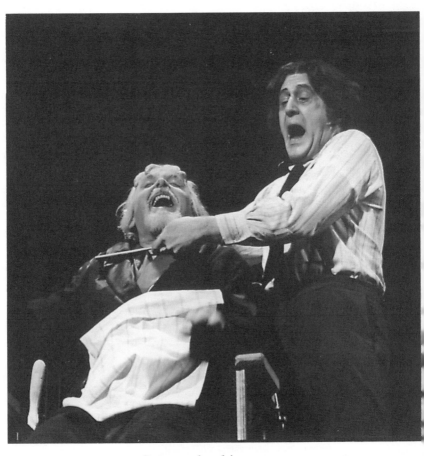

Sweeney has his revenge
Judge Turpin (Edmund Lyndeck) and Sweeney (Len Cariou)

In the Final Sequence, Sweeney (Len Cariou) cradles the body of the dead Beggar Woman (Merle Louise) as a now demented Tobias (Ken Jennings) avenges Sweeney's victims

Dorothy Loudon and George Hearn, who replaced Angela
Lansbury and Len Cariou in the roles of Mrs. Lovett and
Sweeney Todd in the original Broadway production

Rosalind Elias as Mrs. Lovett and Timothy Nolen as
Sweeney Todd in the 1984 New York City Opera production

Bob Gunton as Sweeney Todd and Beth Fowler as Mrs. Lovett in the 1989 Circle-in-the-Square production

Jim Walton (Anthony), Gretchen Kingsley (Johanna), David Barron (Judge Turpin) and Michael McCarty (the Beadle) in the 1989 Circle-in-the-Square production

Sheila Hancock as Mrs. Lovett and Denis Quilley in the original London production

ACT II

Thanks to her increasing prosperity, MRS. LOVETT *has created a modest outdoor eating garden outside the pieshop, consisting of a large wooden table with two benches, a few bushes in pots, birds in cages. At rise, contented customers, one of whom is drunk, are filling the garden, devouring their pies, and drinking ale while* TOBIAS, *in a waiter's apron, drums up trade along the sidewalk. Inside the pieshop,* MRS. LOVETT, *in a "fancy" gown, a sign of her upward mobility, doles out pies from the counter and collects a few on a tray to bring into the garden subsequently.* TODD *is pacing restlessly in the tonsorial parlor. The* BEGGAR WOMAN *hangs around throughout, hungry and ominous.*

TOBIAS:
Ladies and gentlemen,
May I have your attention, perlease?
Are your nostrils aquiver and tingling as well
At that delicate, luscious ambrosial smell?
Yes they are, I can tell.
Well, ladies and gentlemen,
That aroma enriching the breeze
Is like nothing compared to its succulent source,
As the gourmets among you will tell you, of course.

Ladies and gentlemen,
You can't imagine the rapture in store —

141

                    (*Indicating the shop*)
Just inside of this door!
                    (*Beating his usual drum*)
There you'll sample
Mrs. Lovett's meat pies,
Savory and sweet pies,
As you'll see.
You who eat pies,
Mrs. Lovett's meat pies
Conjure up the treat pies
Used to be!

          (TOBIAS *and customers sing, overlapping*)

1ST MAN:
Over here, boy, how about some ale?

2ND MAN:
Let me have another, laddie!

1ST WOMAN:
Tell me, are they flavorsome?

2ND WOMAN:
They are.

3RD WOMAN:
Isn't this delicious?

TOBIAS (*To* 2ND MAN):
Right away.

4TH MAN:
Could we have some service over here, boy?

4TH WOMAN:
Could we have some service, waiter?

3RD MAN:
Could we have some service?

142

2ND *and* 3RD WOMAN:
    Yes, they are.

1ST MAN:
    God, that's good!

2ND MAN:
    What about that pie, boy?

1ST WOMAN:
    Tell me, are they spicy?

2ND WOMAN:
    God, that's good!

5TH WOMAN:
    How much are you charging?

TOBIAS:
    Thruppence.

3RD WOMAN:
    Yes, what about the pie, boy?

4TH WOMAN:
    I never tasted anything so . . .

1ST *and* 5TH WOMAN:
    Thruppence?

5TH MAN:
    Thruppence for a meat pie?

1ST *and* 2ND MAN:
    Where's the ale I asked you for, boy?

TOBIAS:
    Ladies and gentlemen — !

MRS. LOVETT (*Ringing a bell to attract* TOBIAS*'s attention*)
    Toby!

            (*She starts into the garden with a tray of pies*)

TOBIAS:

Coming!

(*To a customer*)

'Scuse me . . .

MRS. LOVETT (*Indicating a beckoning customer*):

Ale there!

TOBIAS:

Right, mum!

(*He runs inside, picks up a jug of ale, whisks back out into the garden and starts filling tankards*)

MRS. LOVETT:

Quick, now!

CUSTOMERS (*Licking their fingers*):

God, that's good!

MRS. LOVETT (*A bundle of activity, serving pies, collecting money, giving orders, addressing each of the patrons individually and with equal insincerity*):

Nice to see you, dearie . . .

How have you been keeping? . . .

Cor, me bones is weary!

Toby — !

(*Indicating a customer*)

One for the gentleman . . .

Hear the birdies cheeping —

Helps to keep it cheery . . .

(*Spying the* BEGGAR WOMAN)

Toby!

Throw the old woman out!

CUSTOMERS:

God, that's good!

(TOBIAS *shoos the* BEGGAR WOMAN *away, but she soon comes back, sniffing*)

144

MRS. LOVETT (*To other customers, without breaking rhythm*):
  What's your pleasure, dearie? . . .
  No, we don't cut slices . . .
  Cor, me eyes is bleary! . . .
    (*As* TOBIAS *is about to pour for a plastered customer*)
  Toby!
  None for the gentleman! . . .
  I could up me prices —
  I'm a little leery . . .
  Business
  Couldn't be better, though —

CUSTOMERS:
  God, that's good!

MRS. LOVETT:
  Knock on wood.
                                    (*She does*)

TODD (*Leaning out of window*):
  Psst!

MRS. LOVETT (*To a customer*):
  Excuse me . . .

TODD:
  Psst!

MRS. LOVETT (*To* TOBIAS):
  Dear, see to the customers.

TODD:
  Psst!

MRS. LOVETT (*Moving toward him*):
  Yes, what, love?
  Quick, though, the trade is brisk.

TODD:
  But it's six o'clock!

MRS. LOVETT:
So it's six o'clock.

TODD:
It was due to arrive
At a quarter to five —

MRS. LOVETT:	TODD:
And it's probably already	And it's six o'clock!
Down the block!	
It'll be here, it'll be here!	I've been waiting all day!
Have a beaker of beer	
And stop worrying, dear.	But it should have been here
Now, now . . .	By now!

CUSTOMERS:
More hot pies!

MRS. LOVETT (*Looking back, agitated at being pulled in two directions*):
Gawd.
                    (*To* TODD, *moving back to the garden*)

Will you wait there,	TODD:
Coolly,	You'll come back
'Cos my customers truly	When it comes?
Are getting unruly.	

                    (*Circulating again in the garden*)
And what's your pleasure, dearie?
                    (*Spilling ale*)
Oops! I beg your pardon!
Just me hands is smeary —
                    (*Spotting a would-be freeloader*)
Toby!
Run for the gentleman!
         (TOBIAS *catches him, collects the money;* MRS. LOVETT
         turns to another customer)
Don't you love a garden?
Always makes me teary . . .

                    (*Looking back at the freeloader*)
Must be one of them foreigners —

CUSTOMERS:

God, that's good that is delicious!
    (*During the following a huge crate appears high on a crane and moves slowly downstage to the tonsorial parlor.* TODD *sees it*)

MRS. LOVETT:

What's my secret?
                      (*To a woman*)
Frankly, dear — forgive my candor —
Family secret,
All to do with herbs.
Things like being
Careful with your coriander,
That's what makes the gravy grander — !

CUSTOMERS:

More hot pies!
    (MRS. LOVETT *hastens into the shop and loads the tray again*)
More hot!
More pies!

TODD (*Out the window*):
Psst!

MRS. LOVETT (*To a customer in the shop*):
Excuse me . . .

TODD:
Psst!

MRS. LOVETT (*To* TOBIAS):
Dear, see to the customers.

TODD:
Psst!

147

MRS. LOVETT:
Yes, what, love?
Quick, though, the trade is brisk.

TODD:
But it's here!

MRS. LOVETT:
It's where?

TODD:
Coming up the stair!

MRS. LOVETT:
(*Holding up the tray*)
I'll get rid of this lot
As they're still pretty hot
And then I'll be there!

TODD:
It's about to be opened
Or don't you care?

No, I'll *be* there!
I will *be* there!
But they'll never be sold
If I let 'em get cold —

But we have to prepare!

(*During the following, the crate is lowered to the tonsorial parlor*)

MRS. LOVETT (*Without pausing for breath, smiling to a customer*):
Oh, and
Incidentally, dearie,
You know Mrs. Mooney.
Sales've been so dreary —
(*Spots the* BEGGAR WOMAN *again*)
Toby — !
(*To the same customer*)
Poor thing is penniless.
(*Indicating* BEGGAR WOMAN, *to* TOBIAS)
What about that loony?

148

(*To the same customer, as* TOBIAS *shoos the* BEGGAR WOMAN
   away again)
Lookin' sort of beery —
Oh well, got her comeuppance —
              (*Hawklike, to a rising customer*)
And that'll be thruppence — and

CUSTOMERS:
(*Singing with mouths full*)   MRS. LOVETT:
God, that's good that is de have you   So she should.
Licious ever tasted smell such
Oh my God what more that's pies good!
         (MRS. LOVETT *goes up to the tonsorial parlor, entering as*
         TODD *opens the crate, revealing an elaborate barber chair*)

TODD *and* MRS. LOVETT (*Swooning with admiration*):
   Oooohhhh! Oooohhhh!
              (*The empty crate swings away on the crane*)

         TODD:
Is that a chair fit for a king,   MRS. LOVETT:
A wondrous neat   It's gorgeous!
And most particular chair?   It's gorgeous!
You tell me where
Is there a seat
Can half compare   It's perfect!
With this particular thing!   It's gorgeous!
I have a few
Minor adjustments   You make your few
To make —   Minor adjustments.
They'll take
A moment.   You take your time,
I'll call you . . .   I'll go see to the customers.

TODD (*Looking at the chair, as* MRS. LOVETT *goes back to the garden*):
   I have another friend . . .

149

TOBIAS:

(*To the customers*)

Is that a pie fit for a king,	MRS. LOVETT:
A wondrous sweet	It's gorgeous!
And most delectable thing?	It's gorgeous!
You see, ma'am, why	
There is no meat	
Pie can compete	It's perfect!
With this delectable	It's gorgeous!
Pie.	

CUSTOMERS (*Simultaneously with above*):
Yum!
Yum!
Yum!

TOBIAS *and* MRS. LOVETT:
The crust all velvety and wavy,
That glaze, those crimps . . .
And then, the thick, succulent gravy . . .
One whiff, one glimpse . . .

CUSTOMERS (*Simultaneously with above*):
Yum! Yum!
Yum! Yum!
Yum! Yum!
Yum! Yum!

TODD:
And now to test
This best of barber chairs . . .

MRS. LOVETT:	
So rich,	TOBIAS:
So thick	So tender
It makes you sick . . .	That you surrender . . .

CUSTOMERS (*Simultaneously with above*):
Yum!

150

Yum!
Yum! Yum!

TODD:
It's time . . .
It's time . . .
Psst!

MRS. LOVETT (*To the customers*):
Excuse me . . .

TODD (*From above*):
Psst!

MRS. LOVETT (*To* TOBIAS):
Dear, see to the customers.

TODD:
Psst!

MRS. LOVETT (*Moving toward him*):
Yes, what, love?

TODD:
Quick, now!

MRS. LOVETT:
Me heart's aflutter — !

TODD:	
When I pound the floor,	
It's a signal to show	MRS. LOVETT:
That I'm ready to go,	When you pound the floor,
When I pound the floor!	Yes, you told me, I know,
	You'll be ready to go
	When you pound the floor —
	Will you trust me?
I just want to be sure.	Will you trust me?
	I'll be waiting below
When I'm certain that you're	For the whistle to blow . . .
In place —	

151

TODD:

I'll pound three times.

> (*He demonstrates on the frame of the window*)

Three times.

> (*He does it again; she nods impatiently*)

And then you —

> (*She knocks at the air two times*)

Three times —

> (*She knocks heavily and wearily on the wall*)

If you —

> (*She knocks again, rolling her eyes skyward*)

Exactly.

CUSTOMERS:

More hot pies!

MRS. LOVETT:

Gawd!

CUSTOMERS:

More hot!

MRS. LOVETT (*Over her shoulder to them*):

Right!

CUSTOMERS:

More pies!

TODD (*Seeing her attention waver*):

Psst!

CUSTOMERS:

More!

MRS. LOVETT:

Wait!

> (*She runs into the bakehouse, which we see for the first time. Upstage are the large baking ovens. Downstage is a butcher's-block table, on which stands a bizarre meat-grind-*

ing machine. In the wall is the mouth of a chute leading down from the tonsorial parlor. Upstage is a trap door leading down to an invisible cellar. While music continues under, TODD *takes a stack of books tied together, puts it in the chair, then pounds three times on the floor.* MRS. LOVETT *responds by knocking three times on the mouth of the chute.* TODD *pulls a lever in the arm of the chair. The chair becomes a slide and the books disappear through a trap. Music. The books reappear from the hole in the bakehouse wall and plop on the floor. The chair resumes its normal position.* MRS. LOVETT *knocks three times excitedly on the chute;* TODD *responds by pounding on the floor three times)*

CUSTOMERS:
    More hot pies!
               (MRS. LOVETT *hurries out of the bakehouse*)
    More hot! More pies!
               (TODD *resumes tinkering happily with the chair*)
    More! Hot! Pies!

MRS. LOVETT *and* TOBIAS (*To the customers*):
    Eat them slow and
    Feel the crust, how thin I (she) rolled it!
    Eat them slow, 'cos
    Every one's a prize!
    Eat them slow, 'cos
    That's the lot and now we've sold it!
               (*She hangs up a "Sold Out" sign*)
    Come again tomorrow — !

MRS. LOVETT (*Spotting something along the street*):
    Hold it —

CUSTOMERS:
    More hot pies!

MRS. LOVETT:
    Bless my eyes — !

(*For she sees the* MAN WITH CAP, *from Act I, approaching the barber sign. He looks up and rings* TODD*'s bell — three times*)

Fresh supplies!

(TODD *leans out, sees the man, beckons him up; the man starts up the steps.* TODD *holds his razor. They both freeze.* MRS. LOVETT *takes down the "Sold Out" sign and turns back to the customers*)

MRS. LOVETT:	TOBIAS:
How about it, dearie?	Is that a pie
Be here in a twinkling!	Fit for a king,
Just confirms my theory —	A wondrous sweet
Toby — !	And most delectable
God watches over us.	Thing?
Didn't have an inkling . . .	You see, ma'am, why
Positively eerie . . .	There is no meat pie —

CUSTOMERS (*Simultaneously with above*):
   Yum!
   Yum!
   Yum!
   Yum! Yum!
   Yum!
   Yum!

MRS. LOVETT (*Spotting the* BEGGAR WOMAN *again*):
   Toby!
   Throw the old woman out!
      (*As* TOBIAS *leads the* BEGGAR WOMAN *off again,* MRS. LOVETT *runs back to the pieshop*)

CUSTOMERS (*Starting with their mouths full, gradually swallowing and singing clearly*):
   God, that's good that is de have you
   Licious ever tasted smell such
   Oh my God what perfect more that's
   Pies such flavor

154

(MRS. LOVETT *relaxes in the pieshop with a mug of ale*)
God, that's good!!!

(*The scene blacks out. The chimes of St. Dunstan's sound softly. It is dawn.* ANTHONY *is searching the streets of London for* JOHANNA)

ANTHONY (*Sings*):
I feel you, Johanna,
I feel you.
Do they think that walls can hide you?
Even now I'm at your window.
I am in the dark beside you,
Buried sweetly in your yellow hair,
Johanna . . .

(*As he continues the search, the light comes up on the tonsorial parlor.* TODD *is seated on the outside stairs, smoking and enjoying the morning. During the following passage, a customer arrives.* TODD *ushers him into the office and into the chair, preparing him for a shave. Throughout the song,* TODD *remains benign, wistful, dream-like. What he sings is totally detached from the action, as is he. He sings to the air*)

TODD:
And are you beautiful and pale,
With yellow hair, like her?
I'd want you beautiful and pale,
The way I've dreamed you were,
Johanna . . .

ANTHONY:
Johanna . . .

TODD:
And if you're beautiful, what then,
With yellow hair, like wheat?

155

I think we shall not meet again —
>*(He slashes the customer's throat)*

My little dove, my sweet
Johanna . . .

ANTHONY:

I'll steal you,
Johanna . . .

TODD:

Goodbye, Johanna.
You're gone, and yet you're mine.
I'm fine, Johanna,
I'm fine!
>*(He pulls the lever and the customer disappears down the chute)*

ANTHONY:

Johanna . . .
>*(Night falls. We see a wisp of smoke rise from the bakehouse chimney, a small trail gradually bellowing out into a great, noxious plume of black. As it thickens, we become aware of* MRS. LOVETT, *in a white nightdress, inside the bakehouse. The oven doors are open and cast a hot light. She is tossing "objects" into the oven. As the music continues under, a figure stumbles into view from the alleyway beside the chimney. It is the* BEGGAR WOMAN, *coughing and spitting and carrying a meager straw pallet, her bed)*

BEGGAR WOMAN (*In a rage, loudly, sings*):

Smoke! Smoke!
Sign of the devil! Sign of the devil!
City on fire!
>*(She tries to interest passers-by but, clearly revolted by her, they move away)*

Witch! Witch!
>>*(Spits at the bakehouse)*

Smell it, sir! An evil smell!
Every night at the vespers bell —
Smoke that comes from the mouth of hell —
City on fire!
(*The smoke trails away as dawn comes up*)
City on fire . . .
Mischief! Mischief!
Mischief . . .

> (*She shuffles off. It is now the next day.* ANTHONY *is
> searching through another part of London.* TODD *is up-
> stairs and looking pleasantly down at the street. A second
> customer arrives and is shown into the shop and prepared,
> as before*)

TODD:

And if I never hear your voice,
My turtledove, my dear,
I still have reason to rejoice:
The way ahead is clear,
Johanna . . .

JOHANNA'S VOICE (*Heard only by* ANTHONY, *she becomes visible
behind bars in a section of the madhouse, Fogg's Asylum, in
which she is incarcerated*):
I'll marry Anthony Sunday . . .
Anthony Sunday . . .

ANTHONY:

I feel you . . .

TODD:

And in that darkness when I'm blind
With what I can't forget —

ANTHONY:

Johanna . . .

TODD:

It's always morning in my mind,

157

My little lamb, my pet,
Johanna . . .

JOHANNA'S VOICE:
I knew you'd come for me one day . . .
Come for me . . . one day . . .

TODD: ANTHONY:
You stay, Johanna —   Johanna . . .
(As they both sing the second syllable of the name, TODD *slashes the second customer's throat so that his mouth opens simultaneously with theirs)*

TODD:
The way I've dreamed you are.
(Dusk gathers; TODD *looks up)*
Oh look, Johanna —
(He pulls the lever and the customer disappears)
A star!

ANTHONY:
Buried sweetly in your yellow hair . . .

TODD (*Tossing the customer's hat down the chute*):
A shooting star!
(Night falls again. Smoke rises. MRS. LOVETT *is again in the bakehouse. The* BEGGAR WOMAN *reappears, coughing fit to kill)*

BEGGAR WOMAN (*Pointing*):
There! There!
Somebody, somebody look up there!
(Passers-by continue to ignore her)
Didn't I tell you? Smell that air!
City on fire!
Quick, sir! Run and tell!
Warn 'em all of the witch's spell!
There it is, there it is, the unholy smell!

158

Tell it to the Beadle and the police as well!
Tell 'em! Tell 'em!
Help!!! Fiend!!!
City on fire!!!
(The smoke thins; dawn rises)
City on fire . . .
Mischief . . . Mischief . . . Mischief . . .
(She makes a feeble curse with her fingers at the bakehouse)
Fiend . . .
(Shrugs, turns pathetically to a passer-by)
Alms . . . alms . . .
(She shuffles off again. During the last section of the song which follows, TODD *welcomes a third customer. He does not kill this one because a wife and child are waiting outside — the child has entered the room and sits on the chest watching* TODD. *By the end of the song* TODD *is again looking softly up at the sky)*

TODD *(Shaving the customer)*:
And though I'll think of you, I guess,
Until the day I die,
I think I miss you less and less
As every day goes by,
Johanna . . .

ANTHONY:
Johanna . . .

JOHANNA'S VOICE:
With you beside me on Sunday,
Married on Sunday . . .

TODD *(Sadly)*:
And you'd be beautiful and pale,
And look too much like her.
If only angels could prevail,
We'd be the way we were,
Johanna . . .

159

ANTHONY:
I feel you . . .
Johanna . . .

JOHANNA'S VOICE:
Married on Sunday . . .
Married on Sunday . . .

TODD (*Cheerfully, looking up at the sky*):
Wake up, Johanna!
Another bright red day!
(*Wistful smile*)
We learn, Johanna,
To say
Goodbye . . .
(*Having completed the shave,* TODD *accepts money from the customer, who leaves with his family*)

ANTHONY (*Disappearing into the distance*):
I'll steal you . . .

(*The scene fades and we see the barred door to Fogg's Asylum. From inside we hear a weird and frightening sound, the cries and gibbering of the inmates. After a moment, rising above the bizarre cacophony, we hear* JOHANNA*'s voice from inside a window, singing a snatch of "Green Finch and Linnet Bird." A few moments later, she breaks off singing and the inmates quieten too as* ANTHONY, *dejected, enters. As he starts across the stage, once again we hear* JOHANNA*'s voice, singing*)

ANTHONY (*Incredulous, overjoyed, stops in his tracks*): Johanna!
(*Calling excitedly up at a window*)
Johanna! Johanna!
(*A male passer-by enters*)
Oh sir, please tell me. What house is this?

PASSER-BY: That? That's Mr. Fogg's Private Asylum for the Mentally Deranged.

160

ANTHONY: A madhouse!

PASSER-BY: I'd keep away from there if I were you.
(*He exits. Once again we hear* JOHANNA's *voice*)

ANTHONY: Johanna! Johanna!
(*He starts beating wildly on the door*)
Open! Open the door !
(*The* BEADLE, *falsely amiable as ever, swaggers on, recognizes him*)

BEADLE: Now, now, friend, what's all this hollering and shouting?

ANTHONY: Oh, sir, there has been a monstrous perversion of justice. A young woman, as sane as you or I, has been incarcerated there.

BEADLE: Is that a fact? Now what is this young person's name?

ANTHONY: Johanna.

BEADLE: Johanna. That wouldn't by any chance be Judge Turpin's ward?

ANTHONY: He's the one. He's the devil incarnate who has done this to her.

BEADLE: You watch your tongue. That girl's as mad as the seven seas. I brought her here myself. So — hop it.

ANTHONY: You have no right to order me about.

BEADLE: No right, eh? You just hop it or I'm booking you for disturbing of the peace, assailing an officer —

ANTHONY: Is there no justice in this city? Are the officers of the law as vicious and corrupted as their masters? Johanna! Johanna!
(*With a little what-can-you-do? shrug, the* BEADLE *blows a whistle. Two policemen hurry on. The* BEADLE *nods to*

161

ANTHONY. *The policemen jump on him but just before they subdue him, he breaks loose and runs away. The policemen start after him)*

BEADLE (*Calling after them*): After him! Get him! Bash him on the head if need be! That's the sort of scalawag that gets this neighborhood into disrepute.

(*As the scene dims we hear first, in the darkness, the shrieks and moans of the asylum inmates. Then loud and raucous, banishing them, we hear the sound of* MRS. LOVETT *singing, as lights come up on her back parlor)*

MRS. LOVETT (*Sitting at the harmonium*):
I am a lass who alas loves a lad
Who alas has a lass
In Canterbury.
'Tis a row dow diddle dow day,
'Tis a row dow diddle dow dee . . .
(*The parlor has been prettied up with new wallpaper and a second-hand harmonium.* TODD *is sitting on the love seat, cleaning his pipe.* MRS. LOVETT *is using the harmonium as a desk. She has a little cash book and is counting out shillings and pennies in piles)*
Nothing like a nice sit down, is there, dear, after a hard day's work?
(*Piling up coins*)
Four and thruppence . . . four and eleven pence . . .
(*Makes a note in the book and does some adding*)
That makes seven pounds nine shillings and four pence for this week. Not bad — and that don't include wot I had to pay out for my nice cheery wallpaper *or* the harmonium . . .
(*Patting it approvingly*)
And a real bargain it was, dear, it being only partly singed when the chapel burnt down.

162

(*Glancing at the unresponsive* TODD)
Mr. T., are you listening to me?

TODD: Of course.

MRS. LOVETT: Then what did I say, eh?

TODD (*Back in his reflections*): There *must* be a way to the Judge.

MRS. LOVETT (*Cross*): The bloody old Judge! Always harping on the bloody old Judge!
              (*She massages his neck*)
We got a nice respectable business now, money coming in regular and — since we're careful to pick and choose — only strangers and such like wot won't be missed — who's going to catch on?
    (*No response; she leans across and pecks him on the lips; sings*)
Ooh, Mr. Todd —
                (*Kisses him again*)
I'm so happy —
                      (*Again*)
I could —
                      (*Again*)
Eat you up, I really could!
You know what I'd like to
Do, Mr. Todd?
                (*Kisses him*)
What I dream —
                (*Again*)
If the business stays as good,
Where I'd really like to go —
                (*No response*)
In a year or so . . .
                (*No response*)
Don't you want to know?

TODD (*Dully*): Of course.

MRS. LOVETT:

Do you really want to know?

TODD (*Feigned enthusiasm*): Yes, yes, I do, I do.
(*Music continues under*)

MRS. LOVETT (*Settling back, after a pause*): I've always had a
dream — ever since I was a skinny little slip of a thing and
my rich Aunt Nettie used to take me to the seaside August
Bank Holiday . . . the pier . . . making little castles in the
sand. I can still feel me toes wiggling around in the briny.
(*She sings*)
By the sea, Mr. Todd,
That's the life I covet;
By the sea, Mr. Todd,
Ooh, I know you'd love it!
You and me, Mr. T.,
We could be alone
In a house wot we'd almost own
Down by the sea . . .

TODD:

Anything you say . . .

MRS. LOVETT:

Wouldn't that be smashing?
(TODD *gives her a pained smile*)
With the sea at our gate,
We'll have kippered herring
Wot have swum to us straight
From the Straits of Bering.
Every night in the kip
When we're through our kippers,
I'll be there slippin' off your slippers
By the sea . . .
With the fishies splashing,

164

By the sea . . .
Wouldn't that be smashing?
Down by the sea —

TODD:
Anything you say,
Anything you say.

MRS. LOVETT:
I can see us waking,
The breakers breaking,
The seagulls squawking:
Hoo! Hoo!
    (*She thinks she's being charming;* TODD *looks at her in terror*)
I do me baking,
Then I go walking
With you-hoo . . .
                    (*Waves*)
You-hoo . . .

I'll warm me bones
On the esplanade,
Have tea and scones
With me gay young blade,
Then I'll knit a sweater
While you write a letter,
                    (*Coyly*)
Unless we got better
To do-hoo . . .

TODD: Anything you say . . .

MRS. LOVETT:
Think how snug it'll be
Underneath our flannel
When it's just you and me
And the English Channel.
In our cozy retreat,

165

Kept all neat and tidy,
We'll have chums over every Friday
By the sea . . .

MRS. LOVETT:

Oh, wait—TODD:

Anything you say . . .

MRS. LOVETT:

Don't you love the weather
By the sea?
We'll grow old together
By the seaside,
Hoo! Hoo!
By the beautiful sea!

(*She speaks, music under*)

Oh, I can see us now — in our bathing dresses — you in a
nice rich navy — and me, stripes perhaps.

(*Sings*)

It'll be so quiet
That who'll come by it
Except a seagull?
Hoo! Hoo!
We shouldn't try it,
Though, till it's legal
For two-hoo!

But a seaside wedding
Could be devised,
Me rumpled bedding
Legitimized.
Me eyelids'll flutter,
I'll turn into butter,
The moment I mutter
"I do-hoo!"

(TODD *gives her a rather appalled glance*)

By the sea, in our nest,
We could share our kippers

With the odd paying guest
From the weekend trippers,
Have a nice sunny suite
For the guest to rest in —
Now and then, you could do the guest in —
By the sea.
Married nice and proper,
By the sea —
Bring along your chopper
To the seaside,

> (*Two slashes*)

Hoo! Hoo!
By the beautiful sea!

> (*Just before the end of the song, she plays a measure of "Here Comes the Bride" on the harmonium. After the song, she nuzzles up to* TODD *on the love seat*)

Come on, dear. Give us a kiss.

> (*Kisses him*)

Ooh, that was lovely. Now, Mr. T., you do love me just a little bit, don't you?

TODD: Of course.

MRS. LOVETT: Then how about it? Of course, there'd have to be a little visit to St. Swithin's to legalize things. But that wouldn't be too painful, would it?

TODD (*Back with his obsession*): I'll make them pay for what they did to Lucy.

MRS. LOVETT (*Almost scolding*): Now, dear, you listen to me. It's high time you forgot all them morbid fancies. Your Lucy's gone, poor thing. It's your Nellie now. Here.

> (*She takes a bon-bon from her purse*)

Have a nice bon-bon.

> (*She kisses him over the bon-bon, has a thought*)

You know, it's seventeen years this Whitsun since my poor

Albert passed on. I don't see why I shouldn't be married in white, do you?

(*From the pieshop, upstage, we hear* ANTHONY *calling*)

ANTHONY (*Off*): Mr. Todd! Mr. Todd!

(*He comes running in*)

I've found her!

TODD (*Jumping up*): You have found Johanna?

ANTHONY: That monster of a Judge has had her locked away in a madhouse!

TODD: Where? Where?

ANTHONY: Where no one can reach her, at Mr. Fogg's Asylum. Oh, Mr. Todd, she's in there with those screeching, gibbering maniacs —

TODD: A madhouse! A madhouse!

(*Swinging around, feverishly excited, buzzing music under*)

Johanna is as good as rescued.

MRS. LOVETT (*Bewildered*): She is?

TODD: Where do you suppose all the wigmakers of London go to obtain their human hair?

MRS. LOVETT: Who knows, dear? The morgue, wouldn't be surprised.

TODD: Bedlam. They get their hair from the lunatics at Bedlam.

ANTHONY: Then you think — ?

TODD: Fogg's Asylum? Why not? For the right amount, they will sell you the hair off any madman's head —

MRS. LOVETT: And the scalp to go with it too, if requested. Excuse me, gentlemen, I'm out!

(Exits)

TODD (*Excitedly, to* ANTHONY): We will write a letter to this Mr. Fogg offering the highest price for hair the exact shade of Johanna's — which I trust you know?

ANTHONY: Yellow.

TODD: Not exact enough. I must make you a credible wig-maker — and quickly.
> *(Sings)*
> There's tawny and there's golden saffron,
> There's flaxen and there's blonde . . .
> *(Speaks)*
> Repeat that. Repeat that!

ANTHONY: Yes, Mr. Todd.

TODD: Well?

ANTHONY:
> There's tawny and there's golden saffron,
> There's flaxen and there's blonde . . .

TODD: Good.
> *(Sings)*

TODD	ANTHONY:
There's coarse and fine,	
There's straight and curly,	There's coarse and fine,
There's gray, there's white,	There's straight and curly,
There's ash, there's pearly,	There's gray, there's white,
There's corn-yellow	There's ash, there's pearly,
Buff and ochre and	There's corn-yellow . . .
Straw and apricot . . .	

(They exit. As the lights dim, a quintet from the company appears and sings)

QUINTET (*Variously*):
Sweeney'd waited too long before —

169

"Ah, but never again," he swore.
Fortune arrived. "Sweeney!" it sang.
Sweeney was ready, and Sweeney sprang.
Sweeney's problems went up in smoke,
All resolved with a single stroke.
Sweeney was sharp, Sweeney was burning,
Sweeney began the engines turning.
Sweeney's problems went up in smoke,
All resolved and completely solved
With a single stroke
By Sweeney!
Sweeney
Didn't wait,
Not Sweeney!
Set the bait,
Did Sweeney! Sweeney! Sweeney!

> (*During this,* TODD *appears on the staircase, accompanied by a strange figure; they enter the tonsorial parlor. We soon realize the figure is* ANTHONY, *disguised as as wigmaker*)

ANTHONY:
(*Finishing his catechism*)
With finer textures,
Ash looks fairer,   TODD:
Which makes it rare,   Good.
But flaxen's rarer —

                                                    No! No!
Yes, yes, I know —   The flaxen's cheaper . . .
Cheaper, not rarer . . .

> (*Music continues under*)

TODD: Here's money.
> (*Hands him purse*)
And here's the pistol.
> (*Hands him a gun*)
For kill if you must. Kill.

ANTHONY: I'll kill a dozen jailers if need be to set her free.

TODD: Then off with you, off. But, Anthony, listen to me once again. When you have rescued her, bring her back here. I shall guard her while you hire the chaise to Plymouth.

ANTHONY: We'll be with you before the evening's out,
                    (*Clasping both* TODD*'s hands*)
Mr. Todd. Oh, thank you — friend.
        (*He hurries off.* TODD *goes to a little writing table, picks up a quill pen and starts to write. The quintet sings what he writes*)

QUINTET (*Variously, as* TODD *writes*):
Most Honorable Judge Turpin —
                    (TODD *pauses reflectively*)
Most Honorable —
                    (TODD *snorts derisively*)
I venture thus to write you this —
                    (*He resumes writing*)
I venture thus to write you this —
                    (*Thinks, choosing the word*)
Urgent note to warn you that the hot-blooded —
                    (*Thinks*)
Young —
                    (*Grunts with satisfaction*)
Sailor has abducted your ward Johanna —
                    (*Stares off sadly*)
Johanna — Johanna —
                    (*Resumes writing*)
From the institution where you —
                    (*Thinks*)
So wisely confined her but,
Hoping to earn your favor,
I have persuaded the boy to lodge her here tonight
At my tonsorial parlor —
                    (*Dips the pen*)
In Fleet Street.
If you want her again in your arms,

Hurry
After the night falls.
> (*He starts to sign, then adds another phrase with a smile*)

She will be waiting.
> (*Reads it over*)

Waiting . . .
> (*Dips pen again, writing carefully*)

Your obedient humble servant,
Sweeney
> (*A flourish of the pen*)

Todd.
> (*Music continues under as* TODD *hurries across the stage to* JUDGE TURPIN*'s house, knocks on the door, which opens, and hands in the letter*)

TODD: Give this to Judge Turpin. It's urgent.

> (*As he disappears, lights come up on the eating garden. It is early evening. The garden is deserted.* MRS. LOVETT *is sitting on the steps knitting a half-finished muffler. The bells of St. Dunstan's sound. After a beat,* TOBIAS *emerges from the shop with a "Sold Out" sign, puts it on the shop door, and goes to* MRS. LOVETT)

TOBIAS: I put the sold-out sign up, ma'am.

MRS. LOVETT: That's my boy.
> (*Holding up the knitting*)

Look, dear! A lovely muffler and guess who it's for.

TOBIAS: Coo, ma'am. For me?

MRS. LOVETT: Wouldn't you like to know!

TOBIAS: Oh, you're so good to me, ma'am. Sometimes, when I think what it was like with Signor Pirelli — it seems like the Good Lord sent you for me.

MRS. LOVETT: It's just my warm heart, dear. Room enough there for all God's creatures.

172

TOBIAS (*Coming closer, hovering, very earnest*): You know, ma'am, there's nothing I wouldn't do for you. If there was a monster or an ogre or anything bad like that wot was after you, I'd rip it apart with my bare fists, I would.

MRS. LOVETT: What a sweet child it is.

TOBIAS: Or even if it was just a man . . .

MRS. LOVETT (*Somewhat uneasy*): A man, dear?

TOBIAS (*Exaggeratedly conspiratorial*): A man wot was bad and wot might be luring you all unbeknownst into his evil deeds, like.

MRS. LOVETT (*Even more wary*): What is this? What are you talking about?

TOBIAS (*Sings*):
Nothing's gonna harm you,
Not while I'm around.

MRS. LOVETT: Of course not, dear, and why should it?

TOBIAS:
Nothing's gonna harm you,
No, sir,
Not while I'm around.

MRS. LOVETT: What do you mean, "a man"?

TOBIAS:
Demons are prowling
Everywhere
Nowadays.

MRS. LOVETT (*Somewhat relieved, patting his head*): And so they are, dear.

TOBIAS:
I'll send 'em howling,

I don't care —
I got ways.

MRS. LOVETT: Of course you do . . . What a sweet, affection-
ate child it is.

TOBIAS:
No one's gonna hurt you,
No one's gonna dare.

MRS. LOVETT: I know what Toby deserves . . .

TOBIAS:
Others can desert you —
Not to worry —
Whistle, I'll be there.

MRS. LOVETT: Here, have a nice bon-bon.
(*Starts to reach for her purse, but* TOBIAS *stays her hand in
adoration*)

TOBIAS:
Demons'll charm you
With a smile
For a while,
But in time
Nothing can harm you,
Not while I'm around.
(*Music continues*)

MRS. LOVETT: What is this foolishness? What're you talking
about?

TOBIAS: Little things wot I've been thinking and wondering
about . . . It's him, you see — Mr. Todd. Oh, I know you
fancy him, but men ain't like women, they ain't wot you
can trust, as I've lived and learned.
(*She looks at him uneasily*)
Not to worry, not to worry,

I may not be smart but I ain't dumb.
I can do it,
Put me to it,
Show me something I can overcome.
Not to worry, mum.

Being close and being clever
Ain't like being true.
I don't need to, I won't never
Hide a thing from you,
Like some.
                    (*Music continues under*)

MRS. LOVETT: Now Toby dear, haven't we had enough foolish
    chatter? Let's just sit nice and quiet for a bit. Here.
    (*She pulls out the chatelaine purse, which is now immedi-
    ately recognizable to the audience as* PIRELLI*'s money purse,
    and starts to fumble in it for a bon-bon*)

TOBIAS (*Suddenly excited, pointing*): That! That's Signor Pirelli's
    purse!
    (MRS. LOVETT, *realizing her slip, quickly hides it*)

MRS. LOVETT (*Stalling for time*): What's that? What was that,
    dear?

TOBIAS: That proves it! What I've been thinking. That's his
    purse.

MRS. LOVETT (*Concealing what is now almost panic*): Silly boy!
    It's just a silly little something Mr. T. gave me for my
    birthday.

TOBIAS: Mr. Todd gave it to you! And how did he get it?
    How did he get it?

MRS. LOVETT: Bought it, dear. In the pawnshop, dear.
    (*To distract him, she lifts the unfinished muffler on its
    needles*)

175

Come on now.
                    (*Sings*)
Nothing's gonna harm you,
Not while I'm around!
Nothing's gonna harm you, Toby,
Not while I'm around.

TOBIAS: You don't understand.
                    (*Sings*)
Two quid was in it,
Two or three —
                    (*Speaks, music continuing*)
The guvnor giving up his purse — with two quid?
                    (*Sings*)
Not for a minute!
Don't you see?
                    (*Speaks, music under*)
It was in Mr. Todd's parlor that the guvnor disappeared.

MRS. LOVETT (*With a weak laugh*): Boys and their fancies!
What will we think of next! Here, dear. Sit here by your
Aunt Nellie like a good boy and look at your lovely muffler. How warm it's going to keep you when the days draw
in. And it's so becoming on you.

TOBIAS (*Sings*):
Demons'll charm you
With a smile
For a while,
But in time
Nothing's gonna harm you,
Not while I'm around!

MRS. LOVETT: You know, dear, it's the strangest thing you coming to chat with me right now of all moments because as I
was sitting here with my needles, I was thinking: "What a
good boy Toby is! So hard working, so obedient." And I
thought . . . know how you've always fancied coming into
the bakehouse with me to help bake the pies?

TOBIAS (*For the first time distracted*): Oh yes, ma'am. Indeed, ma'am. Yes.

MRS. LOVETT: Well, how about it?

TOBIAS: You mean it? I can help make 'em and bake 'em?
(MRS. LOVETT *kisses him again and, rising, starts drawing him back toward the pieshop*)

MRS. LOVETT: No time like the present, is there?
(*She leads him through the pieshop into the bakehouse*)

TOBIAS (*Looking around*): Coo, quite a stink, ain't there?

MRS. LOVETT (*Indicating the trap door*): Them steps go down to the old cellars and the whiffs come up, love. God knows what's down there — so moldy and dark. And there's always a couple of rats gone home to Jesus.
(*She leads him across to the ovens*)
Now the bake ovens is here.
(*She opens the oven doors. A red glow illuminates the stage*)

TOBIAS: They're big enough, ain't they?

MRS. LOVETT: Hardly big enough to bake all the pies we sell. Ten dozen at a time. Always be sure to close the doors properly, like this.
(*Closes doors. Draws him to the butcher's-block table*)
Now here's the grinder.
(*She turns its handle, indicating how it operates*)
You see, you pop meat in and you grind it and it comes out here.
(*Indicates the mouth of the grinder*)
And you know the secret that makes the pies so sweet and tender? Three times. You must put the meat through the grinder three times.

TOBIAS: Three times, eh?

177

MRS. LOVETT: That's my boy. Smoothly, smoothly. And as soon as a new batch of meat comes in, we'll put you to work.

(*She starts for the door back into the pieshop*)

TOBIAS (*Blissful*): Me making pies all on me own! Coo!
(*Noticing her leaving*)
Where are you going, ma'am?

MRS. LOVETT: Back in a moment, dear.
(*At the door she turns, blows him a kiss and then goes into the pieshop, slamming the door behind her and locking it, putting the key in her pocket.* TOBIAS, *too fascinated to realize he has been locked in, starts happily turning the handle of the grinder*)

TOBIAS: Smoothly does it, smoothly, smoothly . . .
(*As he grinds and* MRS. LOVETT *appears at the foot of the stairs to the tonsorial parlor, unseen by her the* BEADLE *enters the back parlor*)

BEADLE: Mrs. Lovett! Mrs. Lovett!

MRS. LOVETT (*Climbing the stairs, looking for* TODD): Mr. Todd! Mr. Todd!

BEADLE (*Notices the harmonium, sits down, and sings from a song book, accompanying himself*):
Sweet Polly Plunkett lay in the grass,
Turned her eyes heavenward, sighing,
"I am a lass who alas loves a lad
Who alas has a lass in Canterbury.
'Tis a row dow diddle dow day,
'Tis a row dow diddle dow dee . . ."

MRS. LOVETT (*Enters, clapping*): Oh, Beadle Bamford, I didn't know you were a music lover, too.

BEADLE (*Not rising*): Good afternoon, Mrs. Lovett. Fine instrument you've acquired.

MRS. LOVETT: Oh yes, it's my pride and joy.

BEADLE (*Sings, as she watches him uneasily*):
Sweet Polly Plunkett saw her life pass,
Flew down the city road, crying,
"I am a lass who alas loves a lad
Who alas has a lass loves another lad
Who once I had
In Canterbury.
'Tis a row dow diddle dow day,
'Tis a row dow diddle dow dee . . ."
       (*He speaks, leafing through the pages*)
Well, ma'am, I hope you have a few moments, for I'm
here today on official business.

MRS. LOVETT: Official?

BEADLE: That's it, ma'am. You see, there's been complaints —

MRS. LOVETT: Complaints?

BEADLE: About the stink from your chimney. They say at
night it's something foul. Health regulations being my
duty, I'm afraid I'll have to ask you to let me take a look.

MRS. LOVETT (*Hiding extreme anxiety*): At the bakehouse?

BEADLE: That's right, ma'am.

MRS. LOVETT (*Improvising wildly*): But, it's locked and . . .
and I don't have the key. It's Mr. Todd upstairs — he's
got the key and he's not here right now.

BEADLE: When will he be back?

MRS. LOVETT: Couldn't say, I'm sure.

BEADLE (*Finds a particular song*): Ah, one of mother's favor-
ites . . .
        (*Sings*)
If one bell rings in the Tower of Bray,

179

Ding dong, your true love will stay.
Ding dong, one bell today
In the Tower of Bray . . .
Ding dong!

TOBIAS (*Joining in from the bakehouse*):
One bell today in the Tower of Bray . . .
Ding dong!

BEADLE (*Stops playing*): What's that?

MRS. LOVETT: Oh, just my boy — the lad that helps me with the pies.

BEADLE: But surely he's in the bakehouse, isn't he?

MRS. LOVETT (*Almost beside herself*): Oh yes, yes, of course. But you see . . . he's — well, simple in the head. Last week he run off and we found him two days later down by the embankment half-starved, poor thing. So ever since then, we locks him in for his own security.

BEADLE: Then we'll have to wait for Mr. Todd, won't we?
(*Sings*)
But if two bells ring in the Tower of Bray,
Ding dong, ding dong, your true love will stray.
Ding dong —
(*Speaks*)
Since you're a fellow music lover, ma'am, why don't you raise your voice along with mine?

MRS. LOVETT: All right.

BEADLE (*Sings*):
If three bells ring in the Tower of Bray . . .
Ding dong!

MRS. LOVETT (*Another "inspiration"*): Oh yes, of course! Mr. Todd's gone down to Wapping. Won't be back for hours. And he'll be ever so sorry to miss you. Why, just the other

180

day he was saying, "If only the Beadle would grace my tonsorial parlor I'd give him a most stylish haircut, the daintiest shave — all for nothing." So why don't you drop in some other time and take advantage of his offer?

BEADLE: Well, that's real friendly of him.
    (*Immovable, he starts to sing another verse*)
If four bells ring in the Tower of —

MRS. LOVETT: Just how many bells are there?

BEADLE: Twelve.
    (*Resumes singing*)
    Ding dong!

MRS. LOVETT (*Resigned*):
    Ding dong!

TOBIAS:
    Ding dong!

BEADLE:
    Ding dong!

BEADLE, MRS. LOVETT *and* TOBIAS:
    Then lovers must pray! . . .
    (*During this,* TODD *enters, reacts on seeing the* BEADLE)

MRS. LOVETT (*With a huge smile of relief*): Back already! Look who's here, Mr. T., on some foolish complaint about the bakehouse or something. He wants the key and I told him you had it. But . . .
    (*Coquettishly, to the* BEADLE)
. . . there's no hurry, is there, sir? Why don't you run upstairs with Mr. Todd and let him fix you up nice and pretty — there'll be plenty of time for the bakehouse later.

BEADLE (*Considering*): Well . . . tell me, Mr. Todd, do you pomade the hair? I dearly love a pomaded head.

MRS. LOVETT: Pomade? Of course! And a nice facial rub with bay rum too. All for free!

BEADLE (*To* TODD): Well, sir, I take that very kindly.

TODD (*Bowing to the* BEADLE): I am, sir, entirely at your — disposal.
>   (*The two men exit.* MRS. LOVETT *hesitates, then speaks*)

MRS. LOVETT: Let's hope he can do it quietly. But just to be on the safe side, I'll provide a little musical send-off.
>   (*She goes to the harmonium, sits down on the stool and starts playing and singing a loud verse of "Polly Plunkett" which continues distantly during the following. In the bakehouse,* TOBIAS *stands by the grinding machine eating a pie. He feels something on his tongue, puts a finger in his mouth and pulls the something out, holding it up for inspection*)

TOBIAS: An 'air! Black as a rook. Now that ain't Mrs. Lovett's 'air. Oh, well, some old black cow probably.
>   (*He continues to eat. He bites on something else, takes it out of his mouth, looks at it*)

Coo, bit of fingernail! Clumsy. Ugh!
>   (*He drops the pie. Bored, he starts around the room, inspecting. He peers at an unidentifiable hole in the wall — the chute. He is baffled by it. As he does so, we hear a strange, shambling, shuffling sound as if a heavy object is falling inside the wall.* TOBIAS *spins around just as the bloody body of the* BEADLE *comes trundling out of the mouth of the chute.* TOBIAS *screams*)

No! Oh no!
>   (*He dashes to the door, tries the handle; it is locked. He starts beating on it*)

Mrs. Lovett! Mrs. Lovett! Let me out! Let me out!
>   (*Wildly he tries to break down the door. It is too solid for him. Whimpering, he stands paralyzed. Then he sees the open trap door leading to the cellar steps. He runs and dis-*

appears down them. In the parlor, MRS. LOVETT *continues to sing and play. After a suitable period, she stops)*

MRS. LOVETT:
. . . With a row dow diddle dow day.
(*As she gets up from the harmonium,* TODD *hurries in)*

TODD: It's done.

MRS. LOVETT: Not yet it isn't! The boy, he's guessed.

TODD: Guessed what?

MRS. LOVETT: About Pirelli. Since you weren't here, I locked him in the bakehouse. He's been yelling to wake the dead. We've got to look after him.

TODD (*Fiercely*): But the Judge is coming. I've arranged it.

MRS. LOVETT: You — worrying about the bloody Judge at a time like this!
(*Grabbing his arm and pulling him toward the door)*
Come on.

(*The scene blacks out. Members of the company appear and sing)*

COMPANY (*Variously*):
The engine roared, the motor hissed,
And who could see how the road would twist?
In Sweeney's ledger the entries matched:
A Beadle arrived, and a Beadle dispatched
To satisfy the hungry god
Of Sweeney Todd,

ALL:
The Demon Barber of Fleet . . .
Sweeney!
. . . Street.
Sweeney! Sweeney!

Sweeney! Sweeney! Sweeney!
Sweeney!
Sweeeeeeneeeeey!

> (*And as they sing the name, they transform themselves into the inmates of Fogg's Asylum, which is now revealed: a huge stone wall and a heavy iron door. Behind the wall, the ragged inmates are crawling, lolling, capering, giggling, shrieking. In the center of them sits* JOHANNA, *her long yellow hair tumbling about her*)

INMATES (*Intoning, chattering, screaming*):
Sweeeeeeeeeeeeeeeneeeeeeeeeeeeey . . .
Sweeneysweeneysweeneysweeney . . .
> (*These moans and humming noises continue under the following, occasionally interrupted by little mad birdlike outbursts of song.* MR. FOGG *enters with* ANTHONY *in his wigmaker's disguise. He carries a huge pair of scissors. Behind them is the asylum wall*)

FOGG: Just this way, sir.

ANTHONY: You do me honor, Mr. Fogg.

FOGG: I agree it would be to our mutual interest to come to some arrangement in regard to my poor children's hair.

ANTHONY: Your — children?

FOGG: We are one happy family here, sir, and all my patients are my children, to be corrected when they're naughty, and rewarded with a sweetie when they're good. But to our business.
> (*As they enter the inside of the asylum, lights come up behind the scrim wall revealing the shadows of the inmates.* MR. FOGG, *as in a shadow play, grabs one female by the hair, pulling her head up for* ANTHONY'*s inspection*)

Here is a charming yellow, a little dull in tone perhaps, but you can soon restore its natural gleam.

(*He drops the head, moves to a man and grabs his head up by the hair*)

Now here! A fine texture for a man and, as you must know, sir, there is always a discount on the hair of a male.

(ANTHONY *has been looking around and has spotted* JOHANNA)

ANTHONY: This one here has hair the shade I seek.

FOGG: Poor child. She needs so much correction. She sings all day and night and leaves the other inmates sleepless.

(*He goes to* JOHANNA *and tugs her, indignantly struggling, across the floor toward* ANTHONY, *by the hair*)

Come, child. Smile for the gentleman and you shall have a sweetie.

(*He brandishes the scissors*)

Now, where shall I cut?

JOHANNA (*Sees* ANTHONY): Anthony!

ANTHONY: Johanna!

FOGG: What is this? What is this?

ANTHONY (*Drawing his pistol*): Unhand her!

FOGG: Why you — !

(*Clutching the scissors, he moves resolutely toward* ANTHONY. ANTHONY *backs away a few steps, but* FOGG *keeps coming*)

ANTHONY: Stop, Mr. Fogg, or I'll fire.

FOGG: Fire, and I will stop.

ANTHONY: I cannot shoot.

(*Losing his nerve,* ANTHONY *drops the gun which* JOHAN-NA *catches in mid-air.* FOGG *moves toward* ANTHONY, *raising the scissors.* JOHANNA, *holding the gun with both hands, shoots* FOGG, *who falls. She drops the gun and together she and* ANTHONY *run out. Compelled by the ener-*

gy released by FOGG's *death, the lunatics tear down the wall and rush out of the asylum, spilling with euphoric excitement onto the street*)

LUNATICS (*In three contrapuntal groups*):
City on fire!
Rats in the grass
And the lunatics yelling in the streets!
It's the end of the world! Yes!
City on fire!
Hunchbacks dancing!
Stirrings in the ground
And the whirring of giant wings!
Watch out!
Look!
Blotting out the moonlight,
Thick black rain falling on the
City on fire!
City on fire!
City on fire!

> (*During this, police whistles sound.* ANTHONY *and* JOHANNA *are still visible hurrying away,* ANTHONY *systematically disposing of the wigmaker's costume, tossing the hat off here, the cloak off there, etc. Throughout,* JOHANNA *is excited and chatty. At one point,* ANTHONY *stops briefly to reconnoiter nervously*)

JOHANNA:
Will we be married on Sunday?
That's what you promised,
Married on Sunday!

> (*Pensively*)

That was last August . . .

> (*He looks at her unbelievingly*)

Kiss me!

> (*He drags her off as the lunatics reappear, this time in two groups*)

186

LUNATICS:
  City on fire!
  Rats in the streets
  And the lunatics yelling at the moon!
  It's the end of the world! Yes!
  City on fire!
  Hunchbacks kissing!
  Stirrings in the graves
  And the screaming of giant winds!
  Watch out! Look!
  Crawling on the chimneys,
  Great black crows screeching at the
  City on fire!
  City on fire!
  City on fire!

  (*As they run off, lights come up on the bakehouse.* TODD,
  holding a lantern, and MRS. LOVETT *enter, looking around
  for* TOBIAS)

MRS. LOVETT (*Sings*):
  Toby!
  Where are you, love?

TODD:
  Toby!
  Where are you, lad?

MRS. LOVETT:
  Nothing's gonna harm you . . .

TODD:
  Toby!

MRS. LOVETT:
  Not while I'm around . . .

TODD (*Opening trap door, peering down*):
  Toby!

187

MRS. LOVETT:

Where are you hiding?
Nothing's gonna harm you,
Darling . . .

TODD:

Nothing to be afraid of, boy . . .
(*Closes the trap door, peers into the darkness*)

MRS. LOVETT:

Not while I'm around.

TODD:

Toby . . .

MRS. LOVETT (*She and* TODD *move upstage, where their voices echo*):

Demons are prowling everywhere
Nowadays . . .

TODD:

Toby . . .

(*They wander off as the lunatics run on*)

LUNATICS:

City on fire!
Rats in the streets
And the lunatics yelling at the moon!
It's the end of the world! Yes!
(*Lights go down on them and come up on the* BEGGAR WOMAN, *peering off through the darkness as if at the pieshop*)

BEGGAR WOMAN:

Beadle! . . . Beadle! . . .
No good hiding, I saw you!
Are you in there still,
Beadle? . . . Beadle? . . .
Get her, but watch it!

She's a wicked one, she'll deceive you
With her fancy gowns
And her fancy airs
And her —
> (*Suddenly shrieking*)

Mischief! Mischief!
Devil's work!
> (*Quietly calling again*)

Where are you, Beadle?
Beadle . . .
> (*As she shuffles off toward the pieshop, lights dim on her and come up on the lunatics*)

LUNATICS:
City on fire!
Rats in the streets
And the lunatics yelling at the moon!
It's the end of the world! Good!
City on fire!
Hunchbacks kissing!
Stirrings in the graves
And the screaming of giant winds!
Watch out! Look!
Crawling on the chimneys,
Great black crows screeching at the
City on fire! . . .

> (*Light comes up on the tonsorial parlor. It is empty for a moment, then* ANTHONY *and* JOHANNA, *who is now dressed in a sailor's uniform, enter; music under*)

ANTHONY: Mr. Todd?

JOHANNA: No one here. Where is this Mr. Todd?

ANTHONY: No matter. He'll be back in a moment, for I trust him as I trust my right arm. Wait for him here — I'll return with the coach in less than half an hour.

JOHANNA: But they are after us still. What if they trace us here? Oh, Anthony, please let me come with you.

ANTHONY: No, my darling, there is no safety for you on the street.

JOHANNA: But dressed in these sailor's clothes, who's to know it is I?

ANTHONY: No, the risk is too great.
> (*As she turns away pouting, he sings*)

Ah, miss,
Look at me, look at me, miss, oh,
Look at me please, oh,
Favor me, favor me with your glance.
Ah, miss,
Soon we'll be, soon we'll be gone
And sailing the seas
And happily, happily wed
In France.
> (*She looks at him and smiles*)

BOTH:
And we'll sail the world
And see its wonders
From the pearls of Spain
To the rubies of Tibet —

JOHANNA:	ANTHONY:
And then home.	And then come home to London.
Some day.	Some day.

> (*They kiss*)

ANTHONY (*Starting out*): And I'll be back before those lips have time to lose that smile.
> (*He rushes off. Music continues under.* JOHANNA *paces. She sees the barber chair, starts to move toward it. During*

190

this, the BEGGAR WOMAN *can be seen below approaching the pieshop. A factory whistle blows.* JOHANNA *gasps, startled, then goes to the chair. She sits in it. Her hand moves to inspect the lever, but before she touches it, the* BEGGAR WOMAN *approaches, calling*)

BEGGAR WOMAN:
Beadle! . . .
Beadle!
Where are you?
Beadle, dear!
Beadle!

JOHANNA (*Simultaneously, jumping up*): Someone calling the Beadle! I knew it!

(JOHANNA *looks wildly around, sees the chest, runs to it and clambers in, closing the lid just as the* BEGGAR WOMAN *comes shuffling on*)

BEGGAR WOMAN (*Vacantly*):
Beadle deedle deedle deedle deedle dumpling,
Beadle dumpling, Be-deedle dumpling . . .

(*Whimpers, growls lasciviously, dimly surveys the room. She sees the chest, feels it; screams and wails. She mimes opening a window, then clutches an imaginary baby to her; pats and rocks it, cradles it and smiles. Lullaby music begins underneath*)

And why should you weep then, my jo, my jing?
Ohh . . .
Your father's at tea with the Swedish king.
He'll bring you the moon on a silver string.
Ohh . . .
Ohh . . .

Quickly to sleep then, my jo, my jing,
He'll bring you a shoe and a wedding ring.
Sing here again, home again,
Come again spring.

191

He'll be coming soon now
To kiss you, my jo, my jing,
Bringing you the moon
And a shoe and a wedding ring.
He'll be coming here again,
Home again . . .

> (*Without warning, leaping in like a thunderbolt,* TODD
> *appears, the razor in his hand; music continues*)

TODD: You! What are you doing here?

BEGGAR WOMAN (*Clutching his arm*): Ah, evil is here, sir. The
stink of evil — from below — from her!

> (*Calling*)

Beadle dear, Beadle!

TODD (*Looking anxiously out the window for the* JUDGE): Out of
here, woman.

BEGGAR WOMAN (*Still clutching his arm*): She's the Devil's
wife! Oh, beware her, sir. Beware of her. She with no pity
. . . in her heart.

TODD: Out, I say!

BEGGAR WOMAN (*Peering dimly at him, sings*):
Hey, don't I know you, mister?

> (*On the street the* JUDGE *approaches the tonsorial parlor*)

TODD (*Seeing him*): The Judge. I have no time.

> (*He turns on the* BEGGAR WOMAN, *slits her throat, puts her*
> *in the chair and releases her down the chute. The* JUDGE
> *enters the room. Music continues under*)

JUDGE: Where is she? Where is the girl?

TODD: Below, your Honor. In the care of my neighbor, Mrs.
Lovett. Thank heavens the sailor did not molest her.
Thank heavens too, she has seen the error of her ways.

JUDGE: She has?

TODD: Oh yes, your lesson was well learned, sir. She speaks only of you, longing for forgiveness.

JUDGE: And she shall have it. She'll be here soon, you say?

TODD (*Sings*):
I think I hear her now.

JUDGE: Oh, excellent, my friend!

TODD:
Is that her dainty footstep on the stair?

JUDGE (*Listening*): I hear nothing.

TODD:
Yes, isn't that her shadow on the wall?

JUDGE: Where?

TODD (*Points*): There!
                    (*The* JUDGE *looks, getting excited*)
Primping,
Making herself even prettier than usual —

JUDGE (*Sings*):
Even prettier . . .

TODD:
If possible.

JUDGE (*Blissful*):
Ohhhhhhh,
Pretty women!

TODD:
Pretty women, yes . . .

JUDGE (*Straightening his coat, patting his hair*): Quickly, sir, a splash of bay rum!

TODD (*Indicating the chair*): Sit, sir, sit.

193

JUDGE (*Settling into the chair, in lecherous rapture*):
  Johanna, Johanna . . .
    (TODD *gets a towel, puts it carefully around him, moves to*
    pick up a bottle of bay rum)

TODD:
  Pretty women . . .

JUDGE: Hurry, man!

TODD:
  Pretty women
  Are a wonder . . .

JUDGE: You're in a merry mood again today, barber.

TODD (*Joyfully*):
  Pretty women!

JUDGE:	
What we do for	TODD:
Pretty women!	Pretty women!

    (*During the following,* TODD *smooths bay rum on the*
    JUDGE*'s face, reaching behind him for a razor*)

Blowing out their candles	Blowing out their candles
Or combing out their hair —	Or combing out their hair,
Then they leave —	
Even when they leave you	Even when they leave,
And vanish, they somehow	They still
Can still remain	Are there,
There with you there . . .	They're there . . .

    (*Music continues under*)

JUDGE: How seldom it is one meets a fellow spirit!

TODD (*Smiling down*): With fellow tastes — in women, at
  least.

JUDGE: What? What's that?

TODD: The years no doubt have changed me, sir. But then, I

194

suppose, the face of a barber — the face of a prisoner in the dock — is not particularly memorable.

JUDGE (*With horrified realization*): Benjamin Barker!
(*The factory whistle blows; the* JUDGE *in terror tries to jump up but* TODD *slashes his throat, then pulls the lever and sends the body tumbling out of sight and down the chute. Music continues. For a long moment,* TODD *stands crouched forward by the chair, exhaling deeply. Then slowly he drops to his knees and even more slowly holds up the razor, gazing at it. He sings*)

TODD:
Rest now, my friend,
Rest now forever.
Sleep now the untroubled
Sleep of the angels . . .
(*Suddenly remembering, speaks*)
The boy.
(*He starts down the stairs. He stops midway, remembering his razor*)
My razor!
(*He starts back up the steps just as* JOHANNA *has climbed out of the chest. She stands frozen*)
You! What are you doing here? Speak!

JOHANNA (*Deepening her voice*): Oh, dear. Er — excuse me, sir. I saw the barber's sign. So thinking to ask for a shave, I —

TODD: When? When did you come in?

JOHANNA: Oh, sir, I beg of you. Whatever I have seen, no man shall ever know. I swear it. Oh, sir, please, sir . . .

TODD: A shave, eh?
(*He turns chair toward her*)
At your service.

JOHANNA: But, sir . . .

TODD: Whatever you may have seen, your cheeks are still as much in need of the razor as before. Sit, sir. Sit.

(TODD *sits* JOHANNA *in the chair. As he goes for the razor, simultaneously the factory whistle blows and* MRS. LOVETT *is heard screaming "Die! Die!" from the bakehouse below.* JOHANNA *jumps up and runs out,* TODD *lunges after her, misses her. She runs away.* TODD *pauses; another scream from the bakehouse sends him running down the stairs, and as he disappears into the pieshop, the company appears*)

COMPANY (*Sings*):
Lift your razor high, Sweeney!
Hear it singing, "Yes!"
Sink it in the rosy skin
Of righteousness!

(*Light comes up on the bakehouse.* MRS. LOVETT *is standing in horror by the mouth of the chute from which the* JUDGE, *still alive, clutches her skirt.* MRS. LOVETT *tries to tug the skirt away from the vise-like grip*)

MRS. LOVETT: Die! Die! God in heaven — die!

(*The* JUDGE*'s fingers relax their grip; he is dead. Panting,* MRS. LOVETT *backs away from him and for the first time notices the body of the* BEGGAR WOMAN. *She pauses*)

You! Can it be? How all the demons of Hell come to torment me!

(*Looks hastily over her shoulder*)

Quick! To the oven.

(*She starts to drag the* BEGGAR WOMAN *to the oven as* TODD *enters, runs to her*)

TODD: Why did you scream? Does the Judge still live?

MRS. LOVETT: He was clutching, holding on to my skirt, but now — he's finished.

(*Continues dragging* BEGGAR WOMAN *to oven*)

196

TODD: Leave them to me. Open the doors.
>   (*He starts to shove her toward the oven*)

MRS. LOVETT (*Clutching the* BEGGAR WOMAN*'s wrists*): No! Don't touch her!

TODD (*Pushing her to the oven doors and leaning down to pick up the* BEGGAR WOMAN): What is the matter with you? It's only some meddling old beggar —
>   (MRS. LOVETT *opens the oven doors and the light from the fire illuminates the* BEGGAR WOMAN*'s face. A chord of music as* TODD *realizes who she is*)
>   Oh no, Oh God . . . "Don't I know you?" she said . . .
>   (*Looks up*)
>   You knew she lived. From the first moment that I walked into your shop you knew my Lucy lived!

MRS. LOVETT: I was only thinking of you!

TODD (*Looking down again, sings*):
>   Lucy . . .

MRS. LOVETT: Your Lucy! A crazy hag picking bones and rotten spuds out of alley ashcans! Would you have wanted to know that was all that was left of her?

TODD (*Slowly looking up*): You lied to me.

MRS. LOVETT (*Sings*):
>   No, no, not lied at all.
>   No, I never lied.

TODD (*To the* BEGGAR WOMAN):
>   Lucy . . .

MRS. LOVETT:
>   Said she took the poison — she did —
>   Never said that she died —
>   Poor thing,
>   She lived —

197

TODD:

I've come home again . . .

MRS. LOVETT:

But it left her weak in the head,
All she did for months was just lie there in bed —

TODD:

Lucy . . .

MRS. LOVETT:

Should've been in hospital,
Wound up in Bedlam instead,
Poor thing!

TODD:

Oh, my God . . .

MRS. LOVETT:

Better you should think she was dead.
Yes, I lied 'cos I love you!

TODD:

Lucy . . .

MRS. LOVETT:

I'd be twice the wife she was!
I love you!

TODD:

What have I done? . . .

MRS. LOVETT:

Could that thing have cared for you
Like me?

(TODD *rises, soft and smiling;* MRS LOVETT *takes a step away in panic. Waltz music starts*)

TODD:

Mrs. Lovett,

You're a bloody wonder,
Eminently practical and yet
Appropriate as always.
As you've said repeatedly,
There's little point in dwelling on the past.

MRS. LOVETT:	TODD:
Do you mean it?	No, come here, my love . . .
Everything I did I swear	
I thought	
Was only for the best,	Not a thing to fear,
Believe me!	My love . . .
Can we still be	What's dead
Married?	Is dead.

(TODD *puts his arm around her waist; she starts to relax in her babbling, and they sway to the waltz, her arms around his neck*)

TODD:

The history of the world, my pet —

MRS. LOVETT:

Oh, Mr. Todd,
Ooh, Mr. Todd,
Leave it to me . . .

TODD:

Is learn forgiveness and try to forget.

MRS. LOVETT:

By the sea, Mr. Todd,
We'll be comfy-cozy,
By the sea, Mr. Todd,
Where there's no one nosy . . .
(*He waltzes her closer to the oven*)

TODD:

And life is for the alive, my dear,

So let's keep living it — !

BOTH:

Just keep living it,
Really living it — !

(*He flings her into the oven. She screams. He slams the doors behind her. Black smoke belches forth. The music booms like an earthquake.* TODD, *gasping, sinks to his knees by the oven doors. Then he rises, moves back to the* BEGGAR WOMAN *and kneels, cradling her head in his arms*)

TODD (*Sings*):

There was a barber and his wife,
And she was beautiful.
A foolish barber and his wife,
She was his reason and his life.
And she was beautiful.
And she was virtuous.
And he was —

(*Shrugs*)

Naive.

(TOBIAS *emerges from the cellar, singing in an eerie voice. His hair has turned completely white*)

TOBIAS:

Pat-a-cake, pat-a-cake, baker man.
Bake me a cake —
No, no,
Bake me a pie —
To delight my eye,
And I will sigh
If the crust be high . . .

(Sees TODD, *speaks*)

Mr. Todd.

(*Notices the* BEGGAR WOMAN)

It's the old woman. Ya harmed her too, have ya? Ya shouldn't, ya know. Ya shouldn't harm nobody.

(*He bends to examine the body;* TODD, *suddenly aware of someone, pushes him violently aside. As* TOBIAS *staggers back and recovers his balance, he notices the razor on the floor, picks it up, plays with it*)

Razor! Razor! Cut, cut, cut cadougan, watch me grind my corn. Pat him and prick him and mark him with B, and put him in the oven for baby and me!

(*Cuts* TODD*'s throat.* TODD *dies across the body of* LUCY *as the factory whistle blows.* ANTHONY, JOHANNA *and* OFFICERS OF THE GUARD *come running on. Seeing the carnage, they all stop*)

You will pardon me, gentlemen, but you may not enter here. Oh no! Me mistress don't let no one enter here, for, you see, sirs, there's work to be done, so much work.

(*While they watch in horror, he moves to the grinding machine and slowly starts to turn the handle*)

Three times. That's the secret. Three times through for them to be tender and juicy. Three times through the grinder. Smoothly, smoothly . . .

(JOHANNA *gives a little cry.* ANTHONY *throws his arm around her. As the group stands watching, still in silence,* TOBIAS *continues to grind. Suddenly, the trap door slaps shut; the light brightens abruptly,* TOBIAS *steps back, looks up and sings . . .*)

Epilogue

TOBIAS:
Attend the tale of Sweeney Todd.
His skin was pale and his eye was odd.

JOHANNA *and* ANTHONY:
He shaved the faces of gentlemen
Who never thereafter were heard of again.

POLICEMEN:
He trod a path that few have trod,

POLICEMEN, JOHANNA *and* ANTHONY:
Did Sweeney Todd,

ALL:
The Demon Barber of Fleet Street.

BEGGAR WOMAN (*Rising*):
He kept a shop in London town,
Of fancy clients and good renown.

JUDGE (*Rising*):
And what if none of their souls were saved?
They went to their maker impeccably shaved

BEGGAR WOMAN, JUDGE *and* POLICEMEN:
By Sweeney,
By Sweeney Todd,

ALL:

The Demon Barber of Fleet Street.

PIRELLI *and* BEADLE (*Entering*):

Swing your razor wide, Sweeney!
Hold it to the skies!
Freely flows the blood of those
Who moralize!

(*The rest of the company enters*)

COMPANY:

His needs are few, his room is bare.
He hardly uses his fancy chair.
The more he bleeds, the more he lives.
He never forgets and he never forgives.
Perhaps today you gave a nod
To Sweeney Todd,
The Demon Barber of Fleet Street.

WOMEN:

Sweeney wishes the world away,
Sweeney's weeping for yesterday,
Hugging the blade, waiting the years,
Hearing the music that nobody hears.
Sweeney waits in the parlor hall,
Sweeney leans on the office wall.

MEN:

No one can help, nothing can hide you —
Isn't that Sweeney there beside you?

COMPANY:

Sweeney wishes the world away,
Sweeney's weeping for yesterday,
Is Sweeney!
There he is, it's Sweeney!
Sweeney! Sweeney!

(*Pointing around the theater*)

There! There! There! There!
There! There! There!
>   (*Pointing to the grave*)
There!
>   (TODD *and* MRS. LOVETT *rise from the grave*)

TODD *and* COMPANY:

Attend the tale of Sweeney Todd!
He served a dark and a hungry god!

TODD:

To seek revenge may lead to hell,

MRS. LOVETT:

But everyone does it, and seldom as well

TODD *and* MRS. LOVETT:

As Sweeney,

COMPANY:

As Sweeney Todd,
The Demon Barber of Fleet . . .
>   (*They start to exit*)
. . . Street!
>   (*The company exits.* TODD *and* MRS. LOVETT *are the last
>   to leave. They look at each other, then exit in opposite direc-
>   tions,* MRS. LOVETT *into the wings,* TODD *upstage. He
>   glares at us malevolently for a moment, then slams the iron
>   door in our faces. Blackout*)

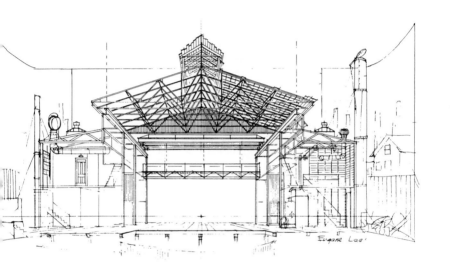

A perspective drawing of the set

The set under construction at the Uris Theatre (*opposite page*) and the completed set (*below*)

MARTHA SWOPE

Costume designs by Franne Lee

SWEENEY TODD

FRANNE LEE '78

TOBIAS "1"   FRANNE LEE '78

MRS LOVETT #2   FRANNE LEE '78

MRS. LOVETT #3

FRANNE LEE '78

JOHANNA

FRANNE LEE '76

MAJOR PRODUCTIONS

Sweeney Todd, the Demon Barber of Fleet Street was first present-ed by Richard Barr, Charles Woodward, Robert Fryer, Mary Lea Johnson, Martin Richards, in association with Dean and Judy Manos, at the Uris Theatre, New York City, on March 1, 1979, with the following cast:

(In order of appearance)

ANTHONY HOPE	Victor Garber
SWEENEY TODD	Len Cariou
BEGGAR WOMAN	Merle Louise
MRS. LOVETT	Angela Lansbury
JUDGE TURPIN	Edmund Lyndeck
THE BEADLE	Jack Eric Williams
JOHANNA	Sarah Rice
TOBIAS RAGG	Ken Jennings
PIRELLI	Joaquin Romaguera
JONAS FOGG	Robert Ousley

THE COMPANY: Duane Bodin, Walter Charles, Carole Doscher, Nancy Eaton, Mary-Pat Green, Cris Groenendaal, Skip Harris, Marthe Ihde, Betsy Joslyn, Nancy Killmer, Frank Kopyc, Spain Logue, Craig Lucas, Pamela McLernon, Duane Morris, Robert Ousley, Richard Warren Pugh, Maggie Task. *Swings* — Heather B. Withers, Robert Henderson.

Directed by Harold Prince
Dance and Movement by Larry Fuller
Production Designed by Eugene Lee
Costumes Designed by Franne Lee
Lighting Designed by Ken Billington
Orchestrations by Jonathan Tunick
Musical Direction by Paul Gemignani

215

The first section of *"The Contest"* (pages 61-62) and the scene in Judge Turpin's house, including the Judge's version of *"Johanna,"* (pages 68-72) were cut in previews for reasons of time.

Sweeney Todd, the Demon Barber of Fleet Street gave its first performance in New York City at the Uris Theatre, where it began previews on February 6, 1979, opened on March 1st and closed on June 29, 1980 after 557 performances and 19 previews.

AWARDS

New York Drama Critics Circle Award — Best Musical

Tony Awards: Best Musical, Best Book of a Musical (Hugh Wheeler), Best Music and Lyrics (Stephen Sondheim), Best Actor in a Musical (Len Cariou), Best Actress in a Musical (Angela Lansbury), Best Direction of a Musical (Harold Prince), Best Scenic Design (Eugene Lee), Best Costume Design (Franne Lee). Also received a Tony nomination for Best Lighting Design (Ken Billington).

Sweeney Todd, the Demon Barber of Fleet Street was first present-
ed in London by Robert Stigwood, in association with David
Land, and by arrangement with Richard Barr, Charles
Woodward, Robert Fryer, Mary Lea Johnson and Martin
Richards, at the Theatre Royal Drury Lane on July 2, 1980
for 157 performances, with the following cast:

SWEENEY TODD	Denis Quilley
MRS. LOVETT	Sheila Hancock
BEGGAR WOMAN	Dilys Watling
TOBIAS	Michael Staniforth
ANTHONY	Andrew C. Wadsworth
JOHANNA	Mandy More
JUDGE TURPIN	Austin Kent
BEADLE BAMFORD	David Wheldon-Williams
PIRELLI	John Aron
JONAS FOGG	Oz Clarke

THE COMPANY: Sylvia Beamish, Michael Bulman, Simon But-
   teriss, Oz Clarke, Linda D'Arcy, Victoria Duncan,
   Katherine Dyson, Mercia Glossop, Andrew Golder, Stuart
   Haycock, Stephen Hill, Marie Jackson, Diane Mansfield,
   Neil Michael, William Relton, Myra Sands, Suzanne
   Sloan, Grant Smith, Rex Taylor Craig, David Urwin

Directed by Harold Prince
Dance and Movement by Larry Fuller
Production Designed by Eugene Lee
Costumes Designed by Franne Lee
Lighting Designed by Ken Billington
Orchestrations by Jonathan Tunick
Production Musical Director, Ray Cook

"Parlor Songs" was deleted and a new song, *"Beggar Woman's Lullaby"* (pages 167-168), was added.

AWARDS

London Standard Drama Award — Best Musical

Society of West End Theatre Awards: Best Musical and Best Actor in a Musical (Denis Quilley). Also received a nomination for Best Actress in a Musical (Sheila Hancock).

Sweeney Todd, the Demon Barber of Fleet Street was presented by the Houston Grand Opera (David Gockley, General Director, John DeMain, Music Director) at the Jones Hall for the Performing Arts, Houston, Texas, June 14-17 and 19-24, 1984 for 10 performances, with the following cast:

ANTHONY HOPE	Cris Groenendaal
SWEENEY TODD	Timothy Nolen
BEGGAR WOMAN	Adair Gockley
MRS. LOVETT	Joyce Castle
JUDGE TURPIN	Will Roy
THE BEADLE	Barry Busse
JOHANNA	Lee Merrill
TOBIAS RAGG	Steven Jacob
PIRELLI	Joseph Evans
JONAS FOGG	Rodney Stenborg

CHORUS: Robert Ard, Lezlie Cole, David Edlund, Lauren Edlund, Mary Jane Ely, Janey Hall, Patricia Hendrickson, Darlene Hitchman, Eileen Koyl, Scott Marshall, Ruth Porter, David Rumpy, Carl Saloga, Robert Sheets, James Sikorski, Margaret Stenborg, Rodney Stenborg, Diana Stoerzbach, James Tinkle, Graydon Vaught

SUPERNUMERARIES: Al Briscoe, Richard Engels, Walt Jaeschke, Bob Mitchell, Julie Stenborg, Mike Talcott, Charles Williams

Conductor, John DeMain
Directed by Harold Prince
Assistant to Mr. Prince, Arthur Masella
Production Designer, Eugene Lee
Costume Designer, Franne Lee
Lighting Designer, Ken Billington
Original Choreography, Larry Fuller

Original Choreography re-created by William Kirk
Sound Design, Jerry O'Brate
Chorus Preparation, Conoley Ballard
Musical Preparation, Stephen Sulich (*Principal Coach*) *and* Craig Bohmler (*Assisting Coach*)
Technical Director, Drew Landmesser

Sweeney Todd, the Demon Barber of Fleet Street was first presented by the New York City Opera (Beverly Sills, General Director, Christopher Keene, Music Director) at the New York State Theatre, New York City, October 11-14 and November 14-18, 1984 for 13 performances, with the following cast:

(In order of appearance)

ANTHONY HOPE	Cris Groenendaal
SWEENEY TODD	Timothy Nolen
BEGGAR WOMAN	Adair Lewis
MRS. LOVETT	Rosalind Elias
JUDGE TURPIN	William Dansby
THE BEADLE	John Lankston
JOHANNA	Leigh Munro
TOBIAS RAGG	Paul Binotto
PIRELLI	Jerold Siena
JONAS FOGG	William Ledbetter

Conducted by Paul Gemignani
Directed by Harold Prince
Assistant to Mr. Prince, Arthur Masella
Scenery Designed by Eugene Lee
Costume Designed by Franne Lee
Lighting Designed by Ken Billington
Choreography by Larry Fuller

Sweeney Todd, the Demon Barber of Fleet Street was revived in London by the Half Moon Theatre, Mile End at the Half Moon Theatre, May 1, 1985 for 33 performances, with the following cast:

ANTHONY HOPE	Christopher Snell
SWEENEY TODD	Leon Greene
BEGGAR WOMAN	Ruth Mayo
MRS. LOVETT	Gillian Hanna
JUDGE TURPIN	Bernard Martin
BEADLE BAMFORD	Edward Clayton
JOHANNA	Eithne Hannigan
TOBIAS RAGG	Andrew Schofield
PIRELLI	John Aron
BIRD SELLER	Judith Street

Directed by Chris Bond
Production Designed by Elen Cairns
Costume Supervisor, Jayne Lambert
Lighting Designer, Jimmy Simmons
Musical Director, Graham Pike
Sound Designer, Tim Foster
Musical Arrangements, Rick Juckes

Sweeney Todd, the Demon Barber of Fleet Street was revived by Circle in the Square (Theodore Mann, Artistic Director, Paul Libin, Producing Director) at the Circle in the Square Theatre, New York City, on September 14, 1989, with the following cast:

JONAS FOGG	Tony Gilbert
POLICEMAN	David E. Mallard
BIRD SELLER	Ted Keegan
DORA	Sylvia Rhyne
MRS. MOONEY	Mary Phillips
ANTHONY HOPE	Jim Walton
SWEENEY TODD	Bob Gunton
BEGGAR WOMAN	SuEllen Estey
MRS. LOVETT	Beth Fowler
JUDGE TURPIN	David Barron
THE BEADLE	Michael McCarty
JOHANNA	Gretchen Kingsley
TOBIAS RAGG	Eddie Korbich
PIRELLI	Bill Nabel

Directed by Susan H. Schulman
Choreography by Michael Lichtefeld
Scenic Design by James Morgan
Costume Design by Beba Shamash
Lighting Design by Mary Jo Dondlinger
Musical Direction and Design by David Krane

This production was originally presented off-off-Broadway by the York Theatre Company (Janet Hayes Walker, Producing Director) at the Church of the Heavenly Rest, March 31-April 29, 1989 for 24 performances. Previews

223

began at the Circle in the Square Theatre on August 5, 1989, and the show opened September 14th and closed February 25, 1990 after 189 performances and 46 previews.

Sweeney Todd, the Demon Barber of Fleet Street was presented on television by RKO/Nederlander and The Entertainment Channel on September 12, 1982, with the following cast:

ANTHONY HOPE	Cris Groenendaal
SWEENEY TODD	George Hearn
BEGGAR WOMAN	Sara Woods
MRS. LOVETT	Angela Lansbury
JUDGE TURPIN	Edmund Lyndeck
THE BEADLE	Calvin Remsberg
JOHANNA	Betsy Joslyn
TOBIAS RAGG	Ken Jennings
PIRELLI	Sal Mistretta
BIRD SELLER	Spain Logue
THE PASSERBY	Walter Charles
JONAS FOGG	Michael Kalinyen

THE COMPANY: Walter Charles, Roy Gioconda, Skip Harris, Michael Kalinyen, Spain Logue, Duane Morris, Patricia Parker, Meredith Rawlins, Stuart Redfield, Candace Rogers, Dee Etta Rowe, Carrie Solomon, Melanie Vaughan, Joseph Warner. *Swings*: Cheryl Mae Stewart, James Edward Justiss, William Kirk.

Executive Producers, Ellen M. Krass *and* Archer King
Produced by Bonnie Burns
Executive in Charge of Production, James Rich, Jr.
Directed for Television by Terry Hughes
Directed for the Stage by Harold Prince
Dance and Movement by Larry Fuller
Production Designed by Eugene Lee
Costumes Designed by Franne Lee

225

Lighting Designed for Television by Bill Klages
Orchestrations by Jonathan Tunick
Musical Conductor, Jim Coleman

The television production was taped at the Dorothy Chandler Pavilion, Los Angeles, where the touring company of *Sweeney Todd* was then performing. This production is available on video cassette: RKO 1002/Image 16008.

SELECTED DISCOGRAPHY

* <u>Original Broadway Cast Recording</u> (1979)
   RCA Records
      LP CBL2-3379 (S); 2 record set
      Cassette CBK2-3379; 2 tape set
      CD 3379-2-RC; 2 disc set
         (all of the above include the Judge's version of *"Johanna,"*
         which was cut from the original Broadway production)
      CD RCD1-5033 (highlights only)

A Stephen Sondheim Evening (1983)
   RCA Records
      LP CBL2–4745 (S); 2 record set
      Cassette CBK2–4745; 2 tape set
   Includes: *"Johanna"*—Cris Groenendaal

Evelyn Lear Sings Sondheim and Bernstein (1981)
   Mercury Records Golden Imports
      LP MR 75136
      Cassette MRI 75136
   Includes: *"Green Finch and Linnet Bird"*

A Stephen Sondheim Collection/Jackie Cain and Roy Kral (1982)
   Finesse Records
      LP FW 38324 (S)
      Cassette FWT 38324
   DRG Records (1990 reissue)
      Casette DSC 25102
      CD DSCD 25102
   Includes: *"Johanna"*—Roy Kral

A Little Sondheim Music/Los Angeles Vocal Arts Ensemble
(1984)
   Angel Records
      LP EMI DS-37347 (S)
      Cassette EMI 4DS-37347
   Includes: *"Prologue: The Ballad of Sweeney Todd"*—Ensemble; *"Green
      Finch and Linnet Bird"*—Delcina Stevenson; *"Pretty Women"*
      —Dale Morich, Michael Gallup; *"By the Sea"*—Janet
      Smith, Michael Gallup; *"Not While I'm Around"*—Paul
      Johnson, Janet Smith

* Winner of the Grammy Award for Best Original Cast Show Album

The Broadway Album/Barbra Streisand (1985)
  Columbia Records
    LP OC 40092
    Cassette OCT 40092
    CD CK 40092
    Includes: *"Not While I'm Around," "Pretty Women"*

A Collector's Sondheim (1985)
  RCA Records
    LP CRL4–5359 (S); 4 record set
    Cassette CRK4–5359; 4 tape set
    CD RCD3–5480; 3 disc set
    Includes: *"Pretty Women"*—Len Cariou, Edmund Lyndeck, Victor
        Garber; *"Epiphany"*—Len Cariou, Angela Lansbuy; *"A Little
        Priest"*—Angela Lansbury, Len Cariou (all three tracks from
        original Broadway cast recording); *"The Ballad of Sweeney
        Todd"* (disco version)—Gordon Grody (an edited version of
        the original disco release by His Majesty's Fish, featuring
        Gordon Grody, RCA Red Seals Disco—PD 11687 [33 1/3
        rpm single])

Sondheim (1985)
  Book-of-the-Month Records
    LP 81–7515 (S); 3 record set
    Cassette 91–7516; 2 tape set
    CD 11–7517; 2 disc set
    Includes: *"The Worst Pies in London"*—Joyce Castle; *"A Little Priest"*
        —Joyce Castle, Timothy Nolen; *"Johanna"*—Chamber En-
        semble; *"Not While I'm Around"*—Steven Jacob

Old Friends/Geraldine Turner Sings the Songs of Stephen
Sondheim (1986)
  Larrikin Records (Australia)
    LP LRF-169
    Cassette TC-LRF-169
        (This album was reissued by Silva Screen Records [London]
        under the title *The Stephen Sondheim Songbook*: LP Song 001,
        Cassette Song C001, CD Song CD001)
    Includes: *"Not While I'm Around"*

Cleo Sings Sondheim/Cleo Laine (1988)
  RCA Records
    LP 7702–1–RC
    Cassette 7702–4–RC
    CD 7702–2–RC
  Includes: *"Not While I'm Around"*

Julie Wilson Sings the Stephen Sondheim Songbook (1988)
  DRG Records
    LP SL 5206
    Cassette SLC 5206
    CD CDSL 5206
  Includes: *"Not While I'm Around"*

The Other Side of Sondheim/Jane Harvey (1988)
  Atlantic Records
    LP 81833-1
    Cassette 81833-4
    CD 81833-2
  Includes: *"Not While I'm Around," "Pretty Women"*

Symphonic Sondheim/Don Sebesky Conducts The London Symphony Orchestra (1990)
  WEA Records (London)
    LP 9031–72 119–1
    Cassette 9031–72 119–4
    CD 9031–72 119–2
  Includes: *"Sweeney Todd Suite,"* (*"The Ballad of Sweeney Todd," "Johanna," "Pretty Women," "A Little Priest," "My Friends"*)

Stephen Sondheim wrote the music and lyrics for *A Funny Thing Happened on the Way to the Forum* (1962), *Anyone Can Whistle* (1964), *Company* (1970), *Follies* (1971), *A Little Night Music* (1973), *The Frogs* (1974), *Pacific Overtures* (1976), *Sweeney Todd, the Demon Barber of Fleet Street* (1979), *Merrily We Roll Along* (1981), *Sunday in the Park with George* (1984), *Into the Woods* (1986) and *Assassins* (1990), the lyrics for *West Side Story* (1957, music by Leonard Bernstein), *Gypsy* (1959, music by Jule Styne) and *Do I Hear a Waltz?* (1965, music by Richard Rodgers), and additional lyrics for a new production of *Candide* (1973, music by Leonard Bernstein). He provided incidental music for the plays *The Girls of Summer* (1956), *Invitation to a March* (1961), *Twigs* (1971) and *The Enclave* (1973). He wrote the music and lyrics for the television production *Evening Primrose* (1966), composed the film scores for *Stavisky* (1974) and *Reds* (1981), wrote songs for the motion pictures *The Seven Percent Solution* (1976) and *Dick Tracy* (1990) and co-authored the film *The Last of Sheila* (1973). He won Tony Awards for his scores for *Company, Follies, A Little Night Music, Sweeney Todd* and *Into the Woods,* and all of these musicals won the New York Drama Critics Circle Award for Best Musical, as did *Pacific Overtures* and *Sunday in the Park with George,* the latter also receiving the Pulitzer Prize in 1985. Mr. Sondheim is on the Council of the Dramatists Guild, having served as its president from 1973 to 1981, was elected to the American Academy and Institute of Arts and Letters in 1983, received the London Evening Standard Award in 1989 for his contribution to the musical theater, and in 1989 was named the first Visiting Professor of Contemporary Theatre at Oxford University.

Hugh Wheeler was a novelist, playwright and screen writer. He wrote more than thirty mystery novels under the pseudonyms Q. Patrick and Patrick Quentin, and four of his novels were transformed into films: *Black Widow, Man in the Net, The Green-Eyed Monster* and *The Man with Two Wives.* For films he wrote the screenplays for *Travels with My Aunt, Something for Everyone, A Little Night Music* and *Nijinsky.* His plays include *Big Fish, Little Fish* (1961), *Look: We've Come Through* (1961) and *We Have Always Lived in the Castle* (1966, adapted from the Shirley Jackson novel), he co-authored with Joseph Stein the book for a new production of the 1919 musical *Irene* (1973), wrote the books for *A Little Night Music* (1973), a new production of *Candide* (1973), *Sweeney Todd, the Demon Barber of Fleet Street* (1979, based on a version of the play by Christopher Bond), and *Meet Me in St. Louis* (adapted from the 1949 M-G-M musical), contributed additional material for the musical *Pacific Overtures* (1976), and wrote a new adaptation of the Kurt Weill opera *Silverlake*, which was directed by Hal Prince at the New York Opera. He received Tony and Drama Desk Awards for *A Little Night Music*, *Candide* and *Sweeney Todd*. Prior to his death in 1987 Mr. Wheeler was working on two new musicals, *Bodo* and *Fu Manchu*, and a new adaptation of *The Merry Widow*.

Christopher Bond has spent the last 35 years acting, directing and writing for the stage and occasionally for television and radio. He lived and worked in Liverpool for 15 years, directing, writing and eventually becoming Artistic Director of both the Everyman and Playhouse Theatres there. He subsequently became Artistic Director of the Half Moon Theatre in London's East End from 1984 to 1989. He has worked extensively in Europe, Scandinavia, Israel and the United States as a director. He has written over 30 pieces for the Theatre including *Sweeney Todd*, *Downright Hooligan*, *Tarzan's Last Stand*, *Judge Jeffreys*, and new versions of *Dracula*, Wycherley's *The Country Wife*, Gay's *The Beggar's Opera* and Verdi's *Macbeth*.